History of
American
Government
and
Law

From a Christian Republic
to a Global Coalition

Printed in the United States of America.

ISBN 1-57558-096-9

Table of Contents

Part I

Part II

Part I

The History

Chapter 1

Government Is Ordained of God
(Romans 13:1)

For centuries and up until the early 1960s America has been blessed above all nations of the earth. We have had more freedom, liberty, prosperity, and privileges than any nation in the world. I can remember when our cities, schools, workplaces, churches, and streets were safe. Children were considered to be a heritage from the Lord. Our public schools made sure our children could read the Word of God, recite the Lord's Prayer, pledge allegiance to our flag, and understood our God-given unalienable rights and freedoms. We not only displayed the Ten Commandments in our schools, courtrooms, and churches, we obeyed them. Evildoers were judged and punished speedily. All nations of the world respected and feared America.

Sadly, the America established by our forefathers has radically changed. We now have same-sex marriages, men and woman having sex change operations, the horrible partial-birth abortion, the selling of aborted baby body parts, the killer abortion drug RU-486, suicide machines, school children killing school children, free condom distribution in our public schools, kiddy porn, satanic rock-and-roll and rap music, and a host of other perversions. In recent years America has been number one in the world in violent crimes, illegal drug use, divorce, teenage pregnancies, and voluntary abortions.

How did America go from being the greatest nation on earth, to being a world leader in such notorious categories? Our foundations have been destroyed. Psalm 11:3 states, "If the foundations be destroyed, what can the righteous do?"

In 1789 our Founding Fathers gave us a not democracy but a republican form of government, according to Article 4, Section 4, of our U.S. Constitution. Do you know what the principles and original intent of our republic

were? Most Americans don't. At one time, every school child in America
knew the answer to this question. An 1836 history book entitled *History of
the United States,* authored by Founding Father Noah Webster, gave students the answer.

> The brief exposition of the constitution of the United States will unfold to
> young persons the principles of republican government; and it is the sincere
> desire of the writer that our citizens should early understand that the genu-
> ine source of correct republican principles is the Bible, particularly the New
> Testament or the Christian religion.[1]

What a strong statement by Mr. Webster, who helped author the U.S. Constitution. "The genuine source of correct republican principles is the Bible."
When was the last time you heard a government or school official say that?

Most Americans think of our country as a democracy. Remember, when
we pledge allegiance to the flag, we pledge allegiance to the republic for
which it stands, not the democracy for which it stands.

Our Founding Fathers never intended for our government to be a democracy, as we can see from the writings of men such as Dr. Benjamin Rush,
who wrote, "A simple democracy is the devil's own government." He also
called a democracy a "mob-ocracy."[2]

Founding Father Fisher Ames, who authored the wording for the First
Amendment, stated, "A democracy is a volcano which conceals the fiery
materials of its own destruction. These will produce an eruption and carry
desolation their way."[3]

Founding Father John Adams stated, "Remember democracy never lasts
long, it soon wastes, exhausts and murders itself. There never was a democracy yet that did not commit suicide."[4] Why did the Founding Fathers detest
a democracy? Because in a democracy, there are no absolutes. For example,
if a majority of the people decide that murder is no longer a crime, it will no
longer be a crime. In our republic, murder is a crime because murder is
always a crime in the Word of God. Hebrews 13:8 states, "Jesus Christ [and
His Word] is the same yesterday and today and forever."

Doctor Jedediah Morse, a Founding Father and educator, the father of
modern geography, had this important statement about Christianity and

our republican government. "Whenever the pillars of Christianity shall be overthrown, our present republican form of government and all the blessings which flow from them must fall with them."[5]

As you are about to find out, it is evident the Bible shaped America more than any other source. You see, our Founding Fathers and early settlers believed government was ordained of God. This sacred belief came directly for Romans 13:1-4. This passage of Holy Scripture also gives the purpose of government and the citizens' responsibility to it. By God's grace I will explain the context of verse 1 and then give applications.

Verse 1 states: "Let every soul be subject unto the higher power. For there is no power but of God, the powers that be are ordained of God."

Notice the last part of this verse "the powers that be are ordained of God." The Greek word for "powers" used here, *exousia,* means authority or magistrate. Today we call magistrates, or the "powers that be," government. Since God Himself ordained government, we need to read His Word, the Bible, which sets forth the purpose, laws, principles, and values for this institution. We can see that government is an institution of God, the same as the family and the church. Did you know that? Sadly, many government officials, citizens, and even pastors and Christians have fallen prey to the myth of "separation of church and state." The phrase "separation of church and state" is not found in our U.S. Constitution, but in Article 142 of the constitution of the former U.S.S.R.

I want to reiterate that the Bible was the foundation of American government and law. This must be done because the revisionists, social engineers, and change agents have rewritten the godly history of America.

Just one example of this is an article from the *Los Angeles Times* entitled "America's Unchristian Beginnings,"[6] written by a college professor of physics. Another article by the same professor stated, "The Founding Fathers were not Christian."[7] Believe it or not, it is easy to refute and expose these claims. Our Founding Fathers were such prolific writers that with a little bit of homework, done at your local library, you can document their true and original intentions. George Washington's writings are contained in ninety-seven volumes; John Adams' in thirty-three volumes; Benjamin Franklin's in forty volumes; and John Quincy Adams' in twenty-three volumes.

Our Founding Fathers required in Article 1, Section 5 of our Constitu-

tion, that everything said in Congress be written into a journal. With this
procedure the people could always be informed on what was said and done. I
am going to show you with these original writings, congressional records,
court cases, and other important documents, proof beyond a shadow of a
doubt that America's beginnings were Christian, as were a vast majority of
our Founding Fathers.

One of the first examples showing the Bible as the foundation of our
government is recorded in *The Journals of the Continental Congress,* September 6, 1774. Boston had just been attacked by the British army. Remember, our Founding Fathers and citizens of the thirteen colonies were still
British citizens under King George. Their own government was now fighting them. Congress responded by making their first official act a call to prayer.
They invited the Rev. Mr. Duché to open Congress the following day with
prayers.[8] Rev. Mr. Duché performed divine service by first reading Psalm
35:1–4:

> Plead my cause, O Lord, with them that strive with me, fight against them
> that fight against me. Take hold of shield and buckler, and stand up for my
> help. Draw out also the spear, and stop the way against them that persecute
> me: say unto my soul, I am thy salvation. Let them be confounded and put
> to shame that seek after my soul: let them be turned back and brought to
> confusion that devise my hurt.

Founding Father John Adams wrote a letter to his wife Abigail describing
what happened after the Word of God was read.

> I never saw a greater effect upon an audience. It seemed as if heaven had
> ordained that Psalm to be read on that morning. After this, Mr. Duché,
> unexpectedly to every body, struck out into an extemporary prayer, which
> filled the bosom of every man present. I must confess, I never heard a better
> prayer. . . .[9]

The painting entitled "The First Prayer in Congress" depicts the effects of
the Bible reading and prayer and is recorded on a famous historical placard
from the Library of Congress. The placard reads:

Washington was kneeling there, and Henry, Randolph, Rutledge, Lee, and Jay, and by their side there stood, bowed in reverence, the Puritan Patriots of New England. . . . They prayed fervently for America, for Congress, . . . and especially for the town of Boston. . . . "It was enough," says Mr. Adams, "to melt a heart of stone. I saw the tears gush into the eyes of the old, grave Pacific Quakers of Philadelphia."[10]

What a testimony!

Our first Congress not only relied on the Bible for the conflict with Great Britain, but it granted approval to print ten thousand copies of the Bible. Up until this time it was illegal for the thirteen colonies to print Bibles in the English language. On September 12, 1782, Congress contracted the printing of these Bibles to Robert Aitken of Philadelphia, Pennsylvania.[11] This edition has come to be known as the "Bible of the Revolution" and was recommended to the inhabitants of the United States. According to the congressional documents accompanying this contract, the Bibles were described to Congress as "a neat edition of the Holy Scriptures for the use of schools."[12] That's correct! Our Founding Fathers wanted to make sure their godly heritage was passed on to the next generation as commanded in Psalm 78.

While serving as president of the United States, Thomas Jefferson, the least religious of our Founding Fathers, became the chairman of the school board for the District of Columbia. One of the main textbooks he proposed for the curriculum was the Bible.[13]

Our Founding Fathers and government not only relied on the Bible to be used in schools, but started Bible societies or groups of people who would print and distribute copies of the Bible. America's first Bible society was the Bible Society of Philadelphia. It was founded in 1791 by Dr. Benjamin Rush.[14] Dr. Rush was a signer of the Declaration of Independence, helped start five colleges and universities, and was an eminent physician and educator, and starter of the American Sunday school program. Thanks to the help of President James Madison, an act was passed by Congress on February 2, 1813, for Dr. Rush's Bible society to mass-produce Bibles. This was American's first mass-produced stereotyped Bible. The Bible Society of Philadelphia is still existence today.[15]

In 1825 the American Tract Society was organized in New York City.

William Jay, the son of Chief Justice John Jay, was the director of the Tract Society which printed and distributed leaflets flyers that were Bible related. Down through the years its membership role has included six U.S. presidents. One of the society's most popular books was *The Tract Primer.*[16] It started with the ABC's. "A is for Adam who was the first man. He broke God's command and thus sin began. C is for Christ, who for sinners was slain. By Him-O how freely!—salvation we gain." The remainder of the primer has forty-eight Bible questions and answers with Scripture references. Another popular tract published by the Tract Society was entitled *A Defense of the Use of the Bible in Schools* by Dr. Benjamin Rush.[17] This tract gave twelve reasons why the Bible should always be used as a school textbook and is still in circulation today.

Our first president, George Washington, took his oath of office with his hand upon an open Bible. This ceremony was symbolic of a covenant or an agreement with God according to the principles, values, and commandments in His Word. For over two centuries each of our presidents has repeated this ceremony.

America's first dictionary of the English language used Bible verses after the definition to help clarify the exact meaning of words. Founding Father Noah Webster authored this dictionary in 1828 and in it we find this definition: "Truth—'. . . Thy Word is truth'(John 17). 'Jesus Christ is called the truth' (John 14). 'To do truth is to practice what God commands' (John 3)."

Today our public schools and the media teach our children and adults that truth is subjective. This is taught by using concepts and phrases such as situation ethics, values clarification, alternative lifestyles, and lest we forget, "politically correct."

Chapter 2

The Bible and Early Martyrs
(A.D. 1200—A.D. 1600)

Today most American citizens and Christians take for granted the freedom and privilege of having a Bible printed in the English language. These same people do not realize our freedoms, rights, and privileges stem from the Bible. Believe me, it was not always this way. Before we go on, I want to give you some inspiring, yet horrifying history of how this godly heritage of having a Bible in your own language, along with its freedoms and liberties, was passed down via our Founding Fathers to you and me.

From the time of the early church in the first century and up to about the twelfth century, most of the persecution against true believers came from the pagan world. After the twelfth century a radical change took place. The Church of Rome, which was the state church, took up the sword against all who opposed their false doctrines, traditions, and pagan superstitions. If anyone did not give complete allegiance to their doctrines, they were labeled "heretics"[1] and deemed treasonous against the state. A person could be convicted as a heretic for reading the Bible in their own common language. At this time, the vast majority of Bibles were written in Latin and chained to the pulpit.[2] Because of the chain, a lay person could not take the Bible out of the building—even if they could read Latin.

An institution or church court called the "Inquisition"[3] was appointed to prosecute heretics. The court included a Grand Inquisition, about twenty officials and executioners. The executioners were to oversee the torture, imprisonment, and public burning and strangling of so-called heretics. The barbaric and gruesome methods used for human confessions are beyond your wildest imagination. Just a few methods included stretching arms and legs on a rack until all the joints were dislocated, crushing the feet and hands in vices, breaking fingers and toes, pulling out teeth, inserting pins under the fingernails and toenails, burning the body with heated red-hot metals, inserting hooks into the fleshy parts of the flesh and then ripping them out, and also cutting off pieces of the flesh. These multitudes that were tortured were then tossed into dungeons where they died a slow, agonizing death. For much more information, you can read the complete story in *The New Foxe's Book of Martyrs* by Harold Chadwick.[4]

In Spain alone, the number condemned as heretics exceeded three million, with about three hundred thousand burned at the stake.[5] This included mothers, fathers, sons, daughters, brothers, and sisters. Untold millions of true Christians were martyred by the most ferocious institution the world has ever known, the Roman Catholic Inquisition.[6] This atrocity would continue for many centuries. No wonder this time period was called the Dark Ages. Why did this true-to-life nightmare happen?

Mainly because it was illegal to read or have a copy of the Bible in the common language.[7] Therefore you were taking the church leaders' word that they were teaching true biblical doctrine and the whole council of God. Hosea 4:6 describes this holocaust perfectly: ". . . My people are destroyed for lack of knowledge. . . ."

Nevertheless, God would always have a remnant to pass on truth from His Word. These God-fearing men we are about to discuss would sow these seeds of truth and pass them on to the next generation, just like Psalm 78 commands. With God's grace we are still reaping that truth today.

A Catholic clergyman named John Wycliffe believed the "scripture must become the common property of all" and that government should be "a government of the people, by the people, and for the people."[8] In 1382 he translated the whole Bible from Latin to English. Wycliffe and his followers, called "Lollards," traveled into towns and villages passing out Bibles and tracts while preaching on street corners and anywhere else they had opportunity. The Catholic Church tried to eradicate this so-called heretical movement. In 1425, over forty years after Wycliffe's death, the church ordered his bones exhumed and burned, along with some two hundred books he had written. His ashes were then cast into the Swift River.[9] Today the truth of Wycliffe taken from the Word of God has been dispersed around the world.

An invention came about in 1455 that would forever change the spreading of knowledge of liberty and biblical truth. The printing press was invented by John Guttenberg. The first book printed by Guttenberg was the Bible.[10] All other recordings before this time had to be done by hand. It would take scribes over a year to hand-copy one Bible. Can you imagine how scarce and expensive they were? Because of the invention of the printing press, kings, and despots would see their power gradually weaken and that of the common people strengthened.

William Tyndale was also one of God's martyrs. He said "If God preserves my life I will cause a boy that driveth a plow to know more of the Scriptures than the pope."[11] Tyndale spent twelve years in exile from his native country, trusting he would not be captured and put to death. In 1525 he translated the New Testament into English for the common man to read. On October 6, 1536, Tyndale was betrayed, arrested, and killed as a heretic. Before he was strangled and burned at the stake he calmly stated, "I call God to record that I have never altered, against the voice of my conscience, one syllable of His Word. Nor would I this day, if all the pleasures, honors, and riches of the earth might be given to me." As Tyndale was fastened to the stake, he cried these final words, "Lord, open the king of England's eyes!"[12] Even though his physical life was extinguished, the flames of liberty would burn brighter than ever. Through Tyndale, truth from the Word of God would be spread to all people throughout England.

Other Christian men such as Martin Luther and John Calvin would continue passing on the same biblical truth that would bring forth the Protestant Reformation. These reformers taught that man was justified by faith alone (Romans 1:17) and *sola scriptura,* a Latin phrase meaning "scripture only,"[13] not the decree of the pope or the king. They also taught *sola fidei,* meaning "faith alone." In other words we do not need the traditions or sacraments of the Catholic Church, but the Scriptures and faith alone.

The next stepping stone in this chain of truth and liberty was the Geneva Bible,[14] translated in 1557 in Geneva, Switzerland. This Bible had some very unique features. First, it was very small (measuring only six inches by eight inches). It was also called a "pocket" Bible. Recall that the Bibles before this time were huge, some being over two feet long, and were called "Pulpit Bibles" because they were chained to the pulpit.

Tyndale's prayers had been answered. Now with the Geneva Bible, everyone from the plow boy to the common man could individually possess, read, and interpret their own Bible without relying on a church official or king.

Second, the Geneva Bible contained extensive marginal commentaries. These commentaries reflected the work and teachings of the reformers, along with Wycliffe and Tyndale. They also denounced the "Divine Rights of Kings" and the authority of the state over the church. The "Divine Rights of Kings" was an ancient pagan doctrine originating at Babylon. This doctrine granted the king divine rule over all the people. The people would have no right to challenge his laws or dictates. Therefore, the king could do no wrong and opposing him was the same as opposing God Himself. The Roman Catholic Church, along with the Church of England, adopted this doctrine of "Divine Rights of Kings" and used Romans 13 out of context to justify it.

Third, the Geneva Bible was the first translation to separate the text into chapters and verses, making quick reference easy. This God-sent translation would become the Bible of the masses. Those masses would eventually include the Pilgrims and Puritans. Originally the Pilgrims and Puritans were part of the Church of England which had cut its ties with the Church of Rome. Sadly there was very little change, if any, that took place in the teachings of the Church of England. In the early 1600s it was still against the law to have a Bible in your own language.[15] The Pilgrims, who were first called Separatists, were hunted and persecuted by both church and civil authorities.

Under the reign of Queen Mary in England, at least two hundred eighty-six Christians were burned at the stake for their beliefs, which earned her the title "Bloody Mary."[16] The first minister of the gospel that "Bloody Mary" had burned at the stake was John Rogers in 1554. His wife and nine small children followed him to the place of execution. Rogers died courageously for the gospel of Jesus Christ.[17] In 1555, John Hooper became the first Puritan to be burned at the stake by "Bloody Mary."[18]

By divine appointment God would bring the Pilgrims and Puritans to America during the 1620s and 1630s. They carried with them the seeds of truth and liberty from the martyrs, reformers, and also the Geneva Bible with its commentaries.

The last tremendous influence I want to tell you about in this chain of

truth and liberty is the book entitled *Lex Rex*.[19] The Reverend Samuel Rutherford authored this book in 1644. The title *Lex Rex* stands for "the law is
prince or king" and was written to refute a pamphlet entitled *Rex Lex* meaning "the king is law," which established the "Divine Right of Kings." Rev.
Rutherford asked forty-four questions concerning the authority and rule of
a king in his book. He then documented from Scripture that all men, including the king, are under the law, not above it. *Lex Rex* was publicly burned in
England and banned in Scotland. Rev. Rutherford was placed under house
arrest and the parliament in Edinburgh condemned him to death.[20] The only
reason he was not executed as a civil rebel was because he died first.

Finally this chain of truth, liberty, and godly heritage was passed on to
our Founding Fathers. They in turn took that same truth and liberty and
drafted our number one document, the Declaration of Independence, and
later the U.S. Constitution and Bill of Rights. I pray we will never forget how
the prison, the scaffold, and the stake were the prices our forefathers had to
pay in order that we might have our present liberty and freedom.

Chapter 3

America Was
Founded as a Christian Nation

So far in our research we have learned from Romans 13:1 that government is ordained of God. We have also documented that the Bible was the original foundation of America. Now let's move on to Romans 13:2: "Whosoever therefore resisteth the power, resisteth the ordinance of God: and they that resist shall receive to themselves damnation [or judgment]."

When anyone resists or opposes "the powers that be," which is lawful government ordained of God, he is also resisting or opposing God. This resistance or opposition is also called civil disobedience. When this happens, the "powers that be," which is lawful government, can pronounce judgment in the form of a fine, prison sentence, or death by execution. However the obedience which the Christian owes to the government is never absolute. We will discuss this subject shortly.

How does a person know if he has resisted or opposed lawful government? By reading and studying the Word of God. Under the original intent of our republican form of government, our American courts used the laws, principles, and values from the Bible for all its decisions.

I want to review some of the eye-opening court cases that took place after the signing of the Declaration of Independence and the Constitution, but first we'll research America's law books.

These first law books, *Blackstone's Commentaries on Law,* were used for about one hundred sixty years by American lawyers, courts, the U.S. Senate, and law schools such as Harvard, Yale, and Princeton. They were used to settle disputes, define words, and examine procedure. They were authored by Sir William Blackstone, a Christian and renowned English jurist who lectured at Oxford. He wrote his famous *Commentaries on Law* in

1766, which opened with a study of the law of God as revealed in the Bible.

In volume I, page 25, Blackstone refutes evolution by stating " . . . When God formed the universe and created matter out of nothing. . . ."

Next, Blackstone states," . . . If our reason [or thinking] were always, as in our first ancestor before his transgression, clear and perfect . . . we would need no other guide."[1] (Blackstone is referring to Adam here in the Genesis account of creation and the fall of man through sin.)

"Providence . . . enforces its laws by . . . direct revelation . . . and they are to be found only in the Holy Scriptures. . . . No human laws should be allowed to contradict these [the Holy Scriptures]."[2] Blackstone also states, "No human laws are of any validity if contrary to this [the Holy Scriptures]."[3]

In the last two paragraphs you have read, Blackstone is defining a phrase found in the preamble to the Declaration of Independence called the "Laws of Nature and of Nature's God." This proves the Declaration of Independence's values and principles are based on the Bible. In the footnotes of this section concerning laws that contradict the Holy Scriptures, Blackstone gives an example from Matthew 2:16. This invalid law or edict was made by King Herod to kill all the children from two years and under.[4] In other words, Blackstone is plainly saying man's laws could never contradict Gods laws written in the Holy Scriptures. If man's laws did contradict God's laws, they were not valid. The Scriptures affirm this in Acts 5:29: ". . . We ought to obey God rather than men." How many laws can you think of in America that contradict God's laws?

Other sections of the sixteen hundred pages of *Blackstone's Commentaries on Law* would use footnotes at the bottom of the pages which gave reference to the Holy Scriptures. Just a few examples include the crime of murder with the footnote referring to Genesis 9:6 and Numbers 35:31[5]; rape— Deuteronomy 22:25[6]; divorce—Matthew 19:9[7]; and kidnapping—Exodus 21:16.[8] There is a whole chapter in *Blackstone's Laws* on "Offenses Against God and Christianity,"[9] including everything from blasphemy and drunkenness to witchcraft, fornication, and obscene prints (pornography). One section under apostasy states:

> . . . If any person educated in the Christian religion, or (a) professing [Christian] . . . shall by writing, printing, teaching, or speaking deny the Christian

> religion to be true, deny the Holy Scriptures to be of divine authority . . . or deny any one of the persons of the Holy Trinity to be God . . . he . . . shall suffer . . . penalties . . . three years imprisonment. . . .[10]

What you just read from America's first law books are very strong doctrinal absolutes and truths. When you read *Blackstone's Commentaries on Law*, it is like having your own personal Bible study.

Earlier I quoted from a school textbook authored by Noah Webster. In the same textbook, *History of the United States,* Noah Webster gave his students another reason why the Bible must be the basis of our Constitution and laws.

> The moral principles and precepts contained in the Scriptures ought to form the basis of all our civil constitutions and laws . . . all the miseries and evils which man suffer from vice, crime, ambition, injustice, oppression, slavery, and war, proceed from their despising or neglecting the precepts contained in the Bible.[11]

Another very strong statement! All of our present-day problems in America such as abortion, homosexuality, crime, pornography, school violence, unconstitutional laws, and all other evils, proceed from despising or neglecting God's laws in the Bible. It is plain to see that our American laws originated from the Word of God.

Now we will review some court cases that used biblical principles and values. After each of these cases we will compare the horrifying and shocking contrasts of court cases from the last few decades of our time.

The first amazing court trial is *Respublica v. John Roberts.*[12] Chief Justice Thomas McKean presided over this Supreme Court case in Pennsylvania on October 5, 1778. Chief Justice McKean was a Founding Father, signer of the Declaration of Independence, governor of Pennsylvania and Delaware and also helped author both states' constitutions.

John Roberts, the defendant, was found guilty of high treason by a jury. He was sentenced to death by hanging. At this time period, a person that was sentenced to death was executed in a few days. The guilty person did not live on "death row" fifteen or twenty years, costing the taxpayers millions of dollars. Justice McKean gave Roberts the following admonition:

> You will probably have but a short time to live. Before you launch into eternity, it behooves you to improve the time that may be allowed you in this world; it behooves you most seriously to reflect upon your past conduct; to repent of your evil deeds, to be incessant in prayers to the great and merciful God to forgive your manifold transgressions and sins, to teach you to rely upon the merit and passion of a dear Redeemer, and thereby to avoid those regions of sorrow, those doleful shades where peace and rest can never dwell; where even hope cannot enter. It behooves you to seek the . . . advice and prayers of pious and good men . . . and to learn the way that leadeth to happiness. May you, reflecting upon these things . . . and be received into company and society of angels . . . and the spirits of just men made perfect, and may you be qualified to enter into the joys of Heaven, joys unspeakable, and full of glory. May God be merciful unto your soul.[13]

This admonition by Justice McKean was nothing less than a Christ-centered altar call and invitation for Roberts to confess and repent of his sins and rely on the Redeemer Jesus Christ for salvation so that he could avoid the sorrows of hell. This case took place in a U.S. court room. Justice McKean was not only a strong Christian like many of our Founding Fathers, but a soul winner. Proverbs 11:30 states ". . . he that winneth souls is wise."

As we jump ahead to the 1990s you will get spiritually sick as we contrast the next few court cases. This district court trial, *Jane Doe v. Santa Fe Independent School District,* was held in Galveston, Texas, on May 5, 1995. A federal judge ordered students not to refer to or pray in Jesus' name at graduation. Can you believe this happened in a U.S. court? Here are excerpts from the courts and presiding federal judge's ruling.

> And make no mistake, the Court is going to have a United States marshal in attendance at the graduation. If any student offends this Court, that student will be summarily arrested and will face up to six months incarceration in the Galveston County Jail for contempt of Court. Anyone who thinks I'm kidding about this order better think again. . . . Anyone who violates these orders, no kidding, is going to wish that he or she had died as a child when this Court gets through with it.[14]

A federal judge tells school graduates that they will get six months in the slammer and wish they had never been born for ending a prayer in Jesus' name! May God help us!

In 1992, a judge ordered that the placard listing the Ten Commandments had to be covered during a murder trial. In this case, *State of Florida v. George Broxson*, the defendant was charged with first-degree murder. The defendant stated he had "the right to be free of any religious pressure" relating to the Ten Commandments, specifically "Do not kill."[15]

I will explain a little later in the presentation how these unconstitutional and illegal rulings have been made.

The next court case set a precedent that confirms America was founded as a Christian nation. In 1799 in the case *Runkel v. Winemiller* the Supreme Court of Maryland made the following declaration: ". . . By our form of government the Christian religion is the established religion and all sects and denominations of Christians are placed upon the same equal footing. . . ."[16] This strong statement was declared only a few years after the signing of the U.S. Constitution and Bill of Rights.

Almost a century later, in 1892, the same declaration would be affirmed in the United States Supreme Court. In this case, *Church of the Holy Trinity v. United States* (Document A), the court gave eighty-seven precedents from America's past history, court cases, charters, and state constitutions why our country was emphatically a Christian nation. Amazingly, I learned more about America's godly heritage from this court case than I did from spending twelve years in a public school. We do not have space to quote the eighty-seven precedents the Supreme Court gave, but I do want to quote three: "Christianity . . . is and always has been a part of the common law. . . . The people of this country profess the general doctrines of Christianity as their rule of faith and practice. . . . We are a Christian people and the morality of the country is deeply engrafted upon Christianity. . . ."[17]

Please keep in mind that our Founding Fathers did not want a national denomination set up to rule America, as was the case in Great Britain. Our Founding Fathers did want God's principles and values from the Holy Scriptures in government and all other institutions, such as the family and education.

Many radical changes started to occur in our courts during the 1960s.

These rulings would chip away the very foundation of America's Christian heritage. The devil's crowd started in Maryland with the Oath of Office, where a candidate must declare a belief in God. In the state Supreme Court case, *Torcaso v. Watkins*,[18] a two hundred-year-old Maryland state constitutional requirement was struck down. Now it would be unconstitutional to require a candidate for public office to declare a belief in God. Four years later, in 1965, the Supreme Court, in *United States v. Seeger*,[19] would extend First Amendment religious protection to virtually every non-Christian religion and belief system under the sun.

According to the Supreme Court, the only qualification for religious protection was for a group to have a "set of beliefs" on the "purpose of the universe." This case, along with other cases would give First Amendment religious protection to atheists,[20] agnostics,[21] infidels,[22] secular humanists,[23] witches or wiccans,[24] Buddhists, and a host of other non-Christian religions.[25]

Unfortunately, judges and lawyers apply today's definition of the word "religion" to its usage in the First Amendment. A contemporary Webster's dictionary from the 1980s give the following definition of religion as "a belief in . . . a supernatural power accepted as the creator . . . of the universe (or) a specific . . . system of this expression." The dictionary then gives as an example "the Buddhist religion." Another modern dictionary gives the following definition for religion: "A set of beliefs concerning the cause, nature, and purpose of the universe."[26] These modern definitions are the work of revisionists, as you are about to read.

For almost two centuries under the First Amendment to the Bill of Rights, the only religion to have protection and tax-exempt status was one that believed in the God of the Bible.

To set the record and facts straight we will use Founding Father Noah Webster's 1828 dictionary of the English language for the original definition of religion.

1. Includes a belief in the being and perfections of God . . .
2. Belief in the revelation of His will to man. . .
3. To obey His Commandments . . .
4. Belief in a state of rewards and punishment . . .
5. Man's accountableness to God. . .

6. True godliness . . .of life with the practice of all moral duties . . .

It is very easy to see that the original definition of religion used by our Founding Fathers was the Christian religion. All other religions, according to Webster's 1828 dictionary, were false religions. If the Webster's dictionary in your home does not have Bible verses after many of the words, you need to throw it away and get a copy of the 1828 original version. I have these dictionaries available. Just write to me!

The next case in our chain of godly heritage was *People v. Ruggles*[27] in 1811. This trial took place in the Supreme Court of New York. The defendant was indicted for blasphemy. In this case, *Blackstone's Commentaries on Law* was used to define blasphemy as "reproaches to our Savior Christ . . . or profane scoffing at the Holy Scriptures."[28] The defendant was sentenced by the Supreme Court of New York to be imprisoned for three months and fined five hundred dollars.[29]

Sadly our courts would later lose the fear and respect of God concerning blasphemy and profanity, starting with school textbooks. The case of *Grove v. Mead School District,*[30] took place in 1985. A high school sophomore was required to read a book entitled *A Learning Tree* in her English class, which contained blasphemy against Jesus Christ. The student filed suit to have the book removed from the curriculum. The court ruled all students taking that class would continue to use the book.

Recall that in *People v. Ruggles* blasphemy carried a prison sentence and fine. Today we not only have blasphemy and profanity in our school textbooks but on our radio stations by "shock jock" Howard Stern, in rock music, on T-shirts, in magazines, TV, movie theaters, on-line computers, and even bumper and window stickers. One of the reasons for this "moral cesspool" and gutter language is because the courts have taken a brand-new direction. Our Founding Fathers' original intent of the First Amendment concerning "freedom of speech" never included blasphemy or profanity. By the way, God gave us the "Ten Commandments" not the "Ten Suggestions."

Blasphemy is a stench and reproach in nostrils of a thrice Holy God. Our courts may allow blasphemers to get away with this sin in this life, but God will not in the next life. Jesus said in Matthew 12:36–37, ". . . That every idle word that men shall speak, they shall give account thereof in the day of judgment. For by thy words thou shall be justified, and by thy words thou shalt be condemned."

In *Commonwealth v. Sharpless*[31] there is a classic description of pornography. This trial took place in the Supreme Court of Pennsylvania in the year 1815. The defendant, Jesse Sharpless, was indicted for showing a pornographic picture to the youth and citizens in his home. The court stated:

[The defendant] . . . in a certain house . . . unlawfully, wickedly, and scandalously did exhibit and show for money, to persons, . . . a certain lewd, wicked, scandalous, infamous, and obscene painting, representing a man in an obscene, impudent and indecent posture with a woman, to the manifest corruption and subversion of youth, and other citizens. . . .

The court continued:

The courts are guardians of public morals, and therefore, have jurisdiction in such cases. . . . The destruction of morality renders the power of the government invalid, . . . it weakens the bands by which society is kept together . . . [the] courts of justice are, or ought to be, the schools of morals. . . .

Once again, the court quoted from *Blackstone's Commentaries on Law* that "lewdness" and "obscene prints" were "offenses against God and religion . . . this is an indictable offense."

This case goes back almost two centuries and is a classic example of the Supreme Court of Pennsylvania "legislating morality." Today, many would vehemently assert that you cannot legislate morality. But if you stop and think about it, all laws legislate morality. The question is, who's morality is it? God's or man's? Remember, "we ought to obey God rather than men" (Acts 5.29).

In spite of America's godly moral heritage, the courts would slide down the slippery slope of pornography. The flood gates of smut would be opened wide in the Supreme Court case *Miller v. California*. In this 1973 case, the court would now use "contemporary community standards"[32] to test the obscenity of pornography. With the stroke of a pen, the absolute standards for

"obscene materials" used in America for almost two centuries would be dis-
carded. Now the community would use " contemporary standards."

Thanks to the Supreme Court and "contemporary standards," we now
have a ten billion dollar a year porn business. (This estimate is sixteen years
old and does not include income from computer porn and dial-a-porn.) This
wicked industry flaunts everything from triple-X porn to kiddy and cyber
porn.[33]

Many television networks have jumped on the porn wagon, including
CBS, NBC, FOX-TV, and MTV. These networks bombard us with pornographic
and lewd behavior, premarital sex, drunkenness, homosexuality, lesbianism,
and foul language. Today you and your family cannot walk into most conve-
nience or grocery stores without being bombarded by racks and racks of
pornography.

To our shame, America is the largest exporter of pornographic material
in the world.[34] Each month pornographers produce approximately four hundred magazines which are viewed by twenty million Americans.[35] Los Angeles, California, has over one hundred porn filmmakers, who produce eighty
percent of the nation's porn films and videos. *Time* magazine estimates the
"dial-a-porn" industry generates $2.4 billion of revenue each year.[36]

AT&T is one of the nation's leading carriers of phone sex, with Americans spending between seven hundred fifty and eight hundred million dollars on phone sex.[37] Meanwhile, Holiday Inn leads their industry by pocket-
ing millions each year from offering "adult porn" films to their guests.[38]

Pornographic web sites that contain "cybersex" record over four million visits per day.[39] The "kiddy porn peddlers" who have warped and twisted
minds, now have at least two hundred sixty-four different magazines.[40] One
is called *Moppets*, with photographs of boys and girls ages three to twelve.
Another is called *Lollitots,* with photographs of girls ages eight to fourteen.

Recall that convicted mass murderer Ted Bundy stated before his execution that pornography played a key role in his brutal murdering of twenty-
four young women.[41]

Justice Department studies show the single largest group exposed to
pornography are adolescents between the ages of twelve and seventeen. As
of May 1995 there were more hard-core porn outlets in this country than
there were McDonald's restaurants. In one study, eighty-six percent of rap-

ists admit to regular use of pornography, while every forty-six seconds a woman is raped in America.

After reading these horrifying and shocking statistics that are ten to fifteen years old, can you believe some people believe pornography is a "victimless crime" and should be protected by "freedom of speech and the press"? The ACLU believes all pornography deserves First Amendment protection.[42]

In 1792, right after the Constitution had been framed, twelve of the thirteen colonies had anti-pornography laws on their books. If obscenity were in fact free speech, these state laws would have been overruled by the U.S. Constitution that had just been framed.

The only solution to pornography is Jesus Christ. He is the only one that can set the captives free. As Christians, we need to be "bringing into captivity every thought to the obedience of Christ" (2 Corinthians 10:5). "For the weapons of our warfare are not carnal, but mighty through God to the pulling down of strong holds" (2 Corinthians 10:4). Philippians 4:8 tells Christians to "think . . . on whatsoever things are true, . . . honest, . . . just, . . . pure, . . . lovely, . . . and of good report. . . ."

Jesus said in Matthew 5: 28-29 ". . . Whosoever looketh on a woman to lust after her hath committed adultery with her already in his heart. And if thy right eye offend thee, pluck it out, and cast it from thee, for it is profitable for thee that one of thy members should perish, and not thy whole body should be cast into hell." Wake up America! Wake up!

Our next case concerning our godly educational heritage was in 1844. In this Supreme Court case, *Vidal v. Girards Executors,* the issue dealt with separating the Bible and Christianity from a college and orphanage in Philadelphia, Pennsylvania. The funds for building this school and orphanage were willed by Mr. Girard, who had died and left his estate, valued at seven million dollars, to the city. There were certain requirements in his will, one of which stated "that no ecclesiastic, missionary, or minister of any sect whatsoever, shall ever hold or exercise any station or duty whatsoever in the said college, nor shall any such person ever be admitted for any purpose, or as a visitor with in the premises." Girard went on to say he wanted only "the purest principles of morality" taught. In other words, he wanted "secular humanism" taught. The famous Daniel Webster, the "Defender of the Constitution" and Walter Jones were the lawyers for the plaintiffs. Jones ar-

gued, "The plan of education proposed is anti-Christian and therefore re-
pugnant to the law." Mr. Webster stated that "Girard's . . . college . . . is not
valuable unless it has a fragrance of Christianity about it. . . ." He then
quoted Deuteronomy 6:7 from the Old Testament and Mark 10:14 from the
New Testament.

Justice Joseph Story delivered the unanimous opinion of the Supreme
Court. He asked the following questions:

> Why may not laymen instruct . . . the general principles of Christianity?
> Why may not the Bible, and especially the New Testament . . . be read and
> taught as a divine revelation in the college? . . . Where can the purest prin-
> ciples of morality be learned so clearly or so perfectly as from the New Tes-
> tament?[43]

The bottom line to this case was that education without Christianity was
anti-Christ and couldn't be permitted—moral principles in government-run
schools must be taught from the Bible. Approximately one and a quarter
centuries later, the same U.S. Supreme Court would hand down a ruling to
ban the official use of the Bible from our American schools.

Amazingly, American schools have had required Holy Bible reading laws
on the books for over two centuries. The first compulsory school law in
America was " The Old Deluder Satan Act" in 1647. The law began, "It
being one chief project of that old deluder, Satan, to keep men from the
knowledge of the Scriptures, as in former times. . . ."[44]

The early American settlers still remembered the times in England when
they were persecuted and kept from the knowledge of the Scriptures. To
make sure this would never happen in America, "The Old Deluder Satan
Act" was passed. Sadly, in 1963 with the Supreme Court case *Abington v.
Schempp*,[45] two hundred and sixteen years of traditional Bible reading in
our American schools was eliminated.

One of the "expert testimonies" at this case stated, "If portions of the
New Testament were read without explanation, they could be and . . . had
been psychologically harmful to the child."[46] The Bible had to be removed
from the school because it could cause brain damage to children.

A year earlier, in the Supreme Court case *Engel v. Vitale,* prayer was removed from our schools. This was accomplished through the myth of "separation of church and state."[47] Recall the phrase "separation of church and state" is not found in our U.S. Constitution, only in the former U.S.S.R. Constitution, Article 142.

In 1980 the "Ten Commandments" were removed from American schools. This U.S. Supreme Court case *Stone v. Graham* gave the following convoluted ruling "If the posted copies of the Ten Commandments are to have any effect at all, it will be to induce schoolchildren to read, meditate upon, perhaps to venerate and obey, the Commandments. . . .[This] is not . . . a permissible objective."[48]

Can you believe that? The kids would no longer be allowed to see the Ten Commandments because they might obey them. Things like "do not steal," "do not lie," and "do not take the Lord's name in vain."

The last few years have been years of mayhem and death in many of our schools. Acts of violence against teachers and students—shootings, beatings, along with other forms of destructive behavior—have become all too commonplace. And we wonder why.

Following is a copy of "The New School Prayer." It was supposedly written by a teenager living in the desert southwest.

Now I sit me down at school,
    Where praying is against the rule.
For this great nation under God,
    Finds mention of Him very odd.
If Scripture now the class recites,
    It violates the Bill of Rights.
And anytime my head I bow,
    Becomes a Federal matter now.

Our hair can be purple, orange, or green,
    That's no offense; it's a freedom scene.
The law is specific, the law is precise.
    Prayers spoken aloud are a serious vice.
For praying in a public hall
    Might offend someone with no faith at all.

In silence alone we must meditate,
God's name is prohibited by the state.

We're allowed to cuss and dress like freaks,
And pierce our noses, tongues and cheeks.
They've outlawed guns, but FIRST the Bible,
To quote the Good Book makes me liable.
We can get our condoms and birth controls,
Study witchcraft, vampires and totem poles.
But the Ten Commandments are not allowed,
No word from God must reach this crowd.

It's scary here I must confess,
When chaos reigns, the school's a mess.
O, Lord, this silent plea I make:
Should I be shot . . . My soul please take![49]

It is time to ask a question. How did all of these unconstitutional and illegal court rulings happen? To find out, may I recommend my hard-hitting video and book entitled *History of American Education: From Harvard Scholars to Worker-Bees of the New World Order.* I cover and document almost four centuries of American education starting with Harvard. You will be blessed and edified with our godly educational heritage. You will also be shocked and horrified at what is being taught in many of our public schools today. This video and book must be viewed and read by you and your children to find out how and why the courts have done a complete flip-flop and taken a brand new direction.

The next to the last court case we will discuss and contrast involves the family. This U.S. Supreme Court case, *Murphy v. Ramsey* dealt with polygamy in the year 1885. The court would once again uphold biblical standards, by stating the following definition of the family, ". . . as consisting in . . . the union for life of one man and one woman in the holy estate of matrimony . . . the sure foundation of all that is stable and noble in our civilization. . . ."[50]

America held the sacred God-ordained institution of marriage found in Genesis 2:24 a priority until recently. Genesis 2:24 states, "Therefore shall a man leave his father and his mother, and shall cleave unto his wife. . . ." The first downward step was in the 1970s with no-fault divorce. It is now easier to modify a marriage contract than to escape from an agreement to purchase a refrigerator. In the spring of 2000 the Vermont Supreme Court legalized same-sex "civil unions." This ruling called, the "Baker Decision," would grant to homosexuals and lesbians all the "rights, privileges and benefits of marriage."[51] This would include the right to adopt children and health benefits.

Governor Howard Dean of Vermont signed into law the "civil unions" as a result of a case brought by two lesbian women. The law went into effect on the first day of July 2000. In a little over six months, fourteen hundred and fifty "civil unions" have been granted. Only three hundred and forty-one were residents of Vermont. Homosexuals and lesbians were flying into Vermont from forty states and nine foreign countries to obtain a "civil union."[52] Their agenda and strategy is to return to their home states and force their local government to honor their Vermont contract. Recently, San Francisco mayor Willie Brown oversaw a ceremony "marrying" more than one hundred gay and lesbian "couples."[53]

Our government schools have stooped so low that they now teach the "ABC's of being gay" to preschoolers in Provincetown, Massachusetts. Miss Cristina, president of the Provincetown PTA, stated, "It is truly a milestone in education." Nearly half of the town's parents are homosexual, as are top school officials.[54] First-graders in California have a new perverted curriculum entitled "Gay-Ed for Tots."[55] In New York, the curriculum entitled "Children of the Rainbow"[56] includes books like *Heather Has Two Mommies, Gloria Goes to Gay Pride,* and *Daddy's Roommate.*

The front page of the January 18, 2000, edition of *USA Today* boldly proclaimed, "Gay Students Stake Their Ground." The article states there are now six hundred gay and lesbian clubs in our American schools. Some of these homosexual students probably were recruited by the two hundred homosexual denominations in America called "Metropolitan Churches."[57]

Once again, to our shame, homosexuals have "stormed the Magic Kingdom" of Walt Disney World in Orlando, Florida. The abominable "Gay Day" is approved by the Disney management and has been repeated once a year since 1990.[58] Recently during "Gay Day" at Disney World, Mickey Mouse and Donald Duck were portrayed as homosexual lovers, with Minnie Mouse and Daisy Duck as lesbians.[59] Disney also supported the lesbian sitcom star, Ellen DeGeneres[60] who was featured on the April 14, 1997, cover of *Time* magazine with the following statement, "Yep, I'm Gay!"

AT&T, MCI, and U.S. Sprint have all jumped on the homosexual bandwagon and helped promote and support this ungodly lifestyle.[61] Are you a customer of AT&T, MCI, or U.S. Sprint? If you are, you are helping promote this immoral and anti-family agenda. Why don't you fight back and help at the same time by switching your long distance telephone service to "Life Line." They are a distinctively Christian telephone company that will return ten percent of your domestic long distance charges to a Christian organization of your choice. I made the switch to Life Line many years ago. Their phone number is 1-800-990-0109. Call them today!

Also to America's disgrace and shame, mainline denominational churches are allowing homosexual couples to say marriage vows in their chapels. The first in history was the Methodist-affiliated Emory University in Atlanta, Georgia. This abomination was approved by the board of trustees, according to Emory chaplain and Methodist minister Miss Susan Henry-Crowe.[62]

Should we be surprised when some of our "churches" do not know right from wrong? We now have homosexuals in the military, Janet Reno has allowed top-secret clearances to homosexuals, the FBI has lifted the ban on homosexual agents, and the office of Federal Personnel Management has officially recognized "Globe," which stands for Gay, Lesbian, or Bisexual Employees Association?[63]

The best way to describe and define these abominable lifestyles is found in America's first law books, *Blackstone's Commentaries on Law.* Our original law books defined "gay rights" as a "crime against nature." Following is the definition students were taught at Harvard, Princeton, Yale, and the University of Virginia:

> [This] . . . crime is more detestable . . . and . . . of a still deeper malignity; the infamous crime against nature, committed either with man or beast . . . the very mention of . . . [the crime against nature] . . . is a disgrace to human nature . . . a crime not fit to be named . . . which leads me to add a word concerning its punishment.

... This the voice of nature and of reason, and the express law of God determined to be capital. Leviticus 20:13–15, "If a man also lie with mankind, as he lieth with a woman, both of them have committed an abomination: they shall surely be put to death; their blood shall be upon them. . . . And if a man lie with a beast, he shall surely be put to death, and ye shall slay the beast."

Blackstone now gives an example from the Bible in Genesis 19: "We have a single instance long before the Jewish dispensation by the destruction of two cities, Sodom and Gomorrah, with fire from heaven, this is a universal precept."[64] Blackstone goes on to say the crime against nature should be treated as a felony. Again and again our law books and courts legislated morality according to God's Word.

The "Father of our Country" and first president of the United States court marshalled a homosexual on March 10, 1778. The incident is recorded in *The Writings of George Washington* and published by the U.S. Government Printing Office.

> At a General Court Marshall . . . Lieutenant Enslin of Colonial Malcom's Regiment tried for attempting to commit sodomy, with John Monhort a soldier; secondly, for perjury in swearing to false accounts, found guilty of the charges exhibited against him, being breaches of the 5th Article 18th Section of the Articles of War and do sentence him to be dismissed the service with Infamy. His Excellency the Commander in Chief [George Washington] approves the sentence and with Abhorrence and Detestation of such Infamous Crime orders Lieutenant Enslin to be drummed out of camp tomorrow morning by all the Drummers and Fifers in the army never to return.[65]

Notice George Washington stated he abhorred and detested this infamous crime. It is hard to believe former President Bill Clinton would permit homosexuals in the military, eight days after being elected. This wicked "don't ask, don't tell," policy[66] would also help undermine and destroy our nation's foundation and character.

One thing is for sure, if our nation does not repent of this wicked sin, the ashes of America will burn hotter than the ashes of Sodom and Gomorrah according to 2 Peter 2:6. "And turning the cities of Sodom and Gomorrah into ashes condemned them with an overthrow, making them an ensample unto those that after should live ungodly."

On August 1, 2001, CNN reported from their web site (*www.cnn.com*) the first gay weddings in Germany. With the implementation of Germany's new law allowing same-sex "marriages," there have been a flurry of same-sex ceremonies. The report tells of two lesbians: "Angelika and Gudrun Pannier, dressed in black tuxedos and white bow ties, exchanged rings and sealed Germany's first legal homosexual union with a kiss on Wednesday. 'It's a great honour to be Germany's first lesbian couple to have a legal partnership,' Angelika, 36, told CNN after the ceremony."

The report went on to relate that "Germany is the latest European country to give legal status to same-sex couples, following Denmark, France, Sweden, Iceland, and Norway. The Netherlands legalized same-sex marriages in April this year, while Belgium and Finland are considering following suit."

In the above statements notice the words "legal," "legal status," and "legalized." The modern world thinks of right and wrong in terms of what man has legalized. Adultery, for example has always been a sin and will always be a sin, but in many places it has been decriminalized. It is now legal and therefore is not viewed as a crime.

There is help and good news for homosexuals, lesbians, bisexuals, etc. First Corinthians 6:11 tells us some of the members of the Corinthian church were in the past effeminate (or homosexual) but were washed, sanctified, and justified in the name of the Lord Jesus, and by the Spirit of our God. We know from this passage homosexuals can repent and turn their lifestyles around through Jesus Christ. Please do not be deceived, the unrighteous including fornicators, idolaters, adulterers, effeminate, abusers of themselves with mankind, thieves covetous, drunkards, revilers, or extortioners shall not inherit the kingdom of God (1 Corinthians 6:9–10). Remember people are not born homosexual or lesbian, it is a choice!

One of the best organizations assisting homosexuals, etc., is "Exodus International North America." They offer information packets on support groups and other resources for former homosexuals as well as friends, parents, and partners of homosexuals. Their phone numbers are 1-888-264-

0877 and 1-206-784-7799. "Exodus" is located in Seattle, Washington, but has many outreach organizations across America.

There are so many other court cases and rulings we could discuss that are unraveling and destroying the moral fiber of the family. The last and most infamous case we will discuss in this chapter is *Roe v. Wade*,[67] which was decided by our Supreme Court in 1973. The court handed down a brand new "constitutional right" for women they called the "right to privacy."[68] In reality, this unconstitutional "right to privacy" was the right to choose how a woman and the abortionist would kill the unborn baby. The court also defined the unborn baby as "property of the mother." Now with a stroke of a pen the Supreme Court would permit a licensed abortion doctor to legally murder a mother's unborn baby during the entire nine months of pregnancy. Throughout the United States two hundred-year history it was against the law in all fifty states to perform abortions on innocent babies.[69]

Listen very closely to what America's first law books, *Blackstone's Commentaries*, had to say about killing an unborn baby. This statement comes from chapter fourteen entitled "Homicide."

> . . . If any person with intent to procure the miscarriage of any woman then being quick with child, unlawfully and maliciously shall administer to her, or cause to be taken by her, any poison or other noxious thing, or shall use any instrument or other means whatever with the like intent, every such offender, and every person counselling, aiding, or abetting such offender shall be guilty of felony, and being convicted thereof, shall suffer death as a felon. . . .[70]

Little did Blackstone know that two centuries later, some of the horrible procedures he described would become legal. Let me explain!

After the Supreme Court case of *Roe v. Wade* in 1973, tens of millions of unborn babies would be aborted. Since *Roe v. Wade*, abortionists have killed over forty million unborn children. The unjust slaughter continues at the present rate of thirty-five hundred children each day.[71] We can compare this slaughter to that of Herod in Matthew 2:16. What a holocaust and travesty! Two decades later, on January 22, 1993, former President Bill Clinton issued an executive order to lift the ban on "fetal tissue" research and harvesting aborted babies.[72] This "Pandora's box" would open the door to the hideous "baby torture" called "partial-birth abortion." This wicked procedure can be compared to the atrocities in Nazi Germany under Hitler. The scissors and suction machine used to kill the baby that is eighty percent born are the assault weapons used.[73] These assault weapons, or instruments as Blackstone named them, are worse than any AK-47. The only differences are the AK-47 is illegal and the scissors and suction machine to kill the four-fifths born baby are not. A better and more truthful name for the "partial-birth abortion" is "murder during delivery." There are thousands of "murder during delivery" or partial birth abortions a year.[74] President Clinton brazenly vetoed a ban on "partial-birth abortion" twice.

The next door to be open in this nightmare of death would be the ghoulish selling of aborted baby parts. These aborted baby parts are put on ice and sent overnight to public universities, pharmaceutical firms, and private research laboratories across America and the world.[75] Some of these institutions are funded by your tax dollars and mine! The taxpayer-funded National Institutes of Health is one of the major traffickers selling baby parts.[76]

I want to tell you about one of the 1999 price lists[77] from one of these institutions. The list gives the exact cost of a baby's body parts. The fee for a liver is $150; a spinal cord, $325; eyeballs, $75; brain, $999; or an entire baby—dead but intact—for $600. One "body part supplier" claimed to fill more than fifteen hundred baby parts orders daily. As you can see, there are "big bucks" to be made from baby parts.What kind of mentally twisted individuals would perform such vile and vicious procedures? The answer is, those who have "the love of money." First Timothy 6:10 states, "For the love of money is the root of all evil. . . ."

After the doors of selling baby parts, partial-birth abortion, and fetal tissue research were opened, doctor-assisted suicide and euthanasia were unleashed on America. In November of 1997 the state of Oregon confirmed the legalization of physician-assisted suicide by a statewide referendum.[78] This Oregon law authorized a physician to give a patient a prescription for a lethal drug to be taken to assist in suicide. There were twenty-seven reported cases of voluntary euthanasia in Oregon in 1999. The message is clear from Oregon—doctors now have a green light to kill their patients. Is Oregon setting a dangerous precedent?

Because this subject is so important, I want to give you a brief history of euthanasia. Euthanasia is defined in the *College Dictionary* as "the putting of a person to death painlessly." That is not euthanasia; it is homicide or murder. Even if it's done painlessly, it is still murder.

Since 400 B.C. the basic ethic of physicians has been the same. This ethic originated from a pagan physician, Hippocrates. It was *primum non nocer,* meaning "first do no harm."[79] Before this time, physicians had two roles—the one of curing and the one of killing.

The moral ethic of Hippocrates was broken first in Germany. In the 1930s euthanasia was permitted in the killing of six thousand disabled and defective children. The methods used were lethal injections of morphine, scopolamine, and cyanide. Later carbon monoxide gas was used because it was more efficient, painless, and the most humane form of death. Soon the adults that were incurably sick and mentally ill were killed on the grounds of compassion. In the first seven months of 1941, over ten thousand mentally ill Germans were given a "painless death" in the "shower room-gas chambers" at Hadamar. The chambers included a fake shower room with benches, and the gas was blown into the water pipes. By the end of 1941, eighty to one hundred thousand Germans were killed by euthanasia.

Euthanasia now set the stage for genocide during the time of Hitler and the Nazi concentration camps. By 1945 there were more than a thousand concentration camps in Germany, Austria, and occupied countries, with seven and a half million people confined therein. Hitler's "gas chambers" were so efficient they could kill ten thousand people in a twenty-four-hour period. The dead bodies were used to make soap from the fat, and boots, briefcases, and bags from the skin. Women's and men's hair was used for the production of felt hats, mattresses, and other products. The ashes and bones were used for fertilizer.[80] These terrible atrocities were all started by opening the door to euthanasia.

In 1984 the Netherlands in Holland opened the door to euthanasia. This is a modern, educated, and industrialized Western nation. A doctor could now kill a patient if the patient requested it. In 1990 a report indicated 25,306 cases of euthanasia. Of these 25,306 cases, 8,750 of them stopped life-prolonging treatment without the patient's consent.[81] That is almost one-third, or every third person being killed without their consent. This is very horrifying and frightening.

It is clear to see where the path that euthanasia and doctor-assisted suicide leads. As already stated, we now have these programs of death in Oregon. Euthanasia will not remain "voluntary" for long.

Another sad example of killing and doctor-assisted suicide is Jack Kevorkian. He helped kill one hundred thirty people with his "suicide machine."[82] Why did our society, courts, and laws allow Kevorkian to help kill one hundred thirty human beings before he was put in prison. He only received thirteen to thirty-two years for one hundred thirty deaths. It is clear to see that America is heading down the same road as Nazi Germany and Holland.

Still another door to be opened in this "Pandora's box" occurred September 28, 2000. The FDA permitted a new and legal way for a woman to kill her unborn baby through the sale of the abortion pill RU-486. Just think, no more clinical visits, and a woman could take this abortion pill in the privacy of her home where no one would ever know. A better and more truthful name for RU-486 is "baby killer poison." Recall our first law books also used the term "poison."

There are six things God hates in Proverbs 6:16–19. One of those things is ". . . the hands that shed innocent blood." God hates aborting innocent babies and their blood. He does not hate the woman or abortionist, only their sin. I might add there is forgiveness in Jesus Christ for mothers, doctors, and nurses who have committed these terrible crimes.

The latest onslaught on innocent human life is the "harvesting" of stem cells from human embryos. When the researcher cuts open the embryo to extract stem cells, the baby (which is called a "blastocyst") is killed. This unholy harvesting is nothing more than an industry of death. God's Word teaches in Psalm 51:5, 139:13–16, and Jeremiah 1:5 that life begins at conception.

Believe it or not, laboratories in Virginia and Massachusetts are cloning embryos. What kind of Frankenstein experiments, procedures, and research will be allowed in the future? Presently it is illegal to experiment on cloning human beings. So far scientists have cloned sheep, mice, goats, pigs, and cows. According to the front page story of the August 8, 2001, edition of *USA Today,* three maverick researchers expect to begin human cloning efforts in November. At an undisclosed location outside the U.S.A., Severino Antinori of the International Associated Research Institute in Italy and Panos Zavos, director of the Andrology Institute of America, told the National Academy of Sciences panel that they are recruiting infertile couples for the cloning project. The same article stated Brigitte Boisselier, director of Clonaid, a private company associated with the Raelian space alien cult, said she will also clone humans in the near future.

When you review the track record of our American courts concerning abortion, homosexuals, civil union marriages, legalization of pornography, and euthanasia, along with a host of other vices, it will only be a short time till cloning humans will be permitted by law.

Chapter 4

If the Foundations Be Destroyed?
(Psalm 11:3)

It's time to ask a question. When and how did our American courts take a new direction that is contrary to its original intent and Christian foundations? I want to give you seven main reasons.

1. In 1870 a man by the name of Christopher Langdell became the dean of Harvard Law School. Langdell believed wholeheartedly in Charles Darwin's theory of evolution. He also believed that as man evolved, his laws must also evolve. Langdell taught that judges should guide the evolution of the Constitution. This method as he introduced it at Harvard was known as "case law."[1]

    This "case law" method would allow judges to interpret the U.S. Constitution and Bill of Rights as they believed it should be interpreted. This new direction completely ignored our Founding Fathers' original intent, history, and Christian foundations. Our Founding Fathers used "common law" to interpret the Constitution and Bill of Rights. This interpretation was simply called "biblical law." We learned this from *Blackstone's Commentaries.* This "case law" method caused such an uproar among the other law professors at Harvard that many resigned. Langdell then filled those vacant positions with law professors who held to his case law method. By the 1930s the seeds of case law had been sown in the law students' hearts for many decades. The harvest of corruption finally came and *Blackstone's Commentaries,* based on biblical law, was discarded. Langdell was succeeded by Roscoe Pound, who carried the torch of "case law" to new heights in the law schools and educational arenas of America.[2] The foundations were now being destroyed.

Other colleges and universities would now follow in Harvard's footsteps.

2. In 1940, in the case *Cantwell v. Connecticut*,[3] the U.S. Supreme Court unconstitutionally applied the First Amendment Free Exercise Clause to the states by redefining the intent of the Fourteenth Amendment. The courts now describe this ruling as "selective incorporation."[4] Prior to this ruling, the U.S. Supreme Court never had jurisdiction over First Amendment issues. These issues included freedom of religion, speech, press, assembly, and petition of government. This unconstitutional jurisdiction can be documented and proven by simply reading the Tenth Amendment to the Bill of Rights. "The powers not delegated to the United States by the Constitution, nor prohibited by it to the State, are reserved to the states respectively, or to the people."

This decision of applying the First Amendment to the states would establish a precedent and would be followed by more such cases. Now America could be pushed even further toward a secularist society.

3. In the 1960s, the myth of "separation of church and state" was used by the courts. As previously stated, this phrase is not found in our U.S. Constitution, but is found in Article 142 of the former U.S.S.R. Constitution. Our revisionist courts would now use a secular humanist agenda.

4. About this time many subversive organizations started to come out of the shadows and into the public arena. These anti-American groups would use deceptive names, such as the American Civil Liberties Union. Roger Baldwin[5] was the founder of this organization, which was a front for the Communist Party. He also served a prison sentence for sedition. A few of the ACLU official positions which impact you and your family include: legalization of child pornography, legalization of drugs, abortion on demand, mandatory sex education in schools, and public demonstrations for Nazi and Communist events. The ACLU opposes voluntary public school prayer, tax exemption for churches, religious displays in public, parental consent laws, and home schooling.

Another very deceptive organization is Planned Parenthood, founded in 1915 by Margaret Sanger.[6] The original name of Planned Parenthood was the National Birth Control League. It was not until 1942 and three name changes later that it became known as Planned Parenthood. In her first newspaper, *The Woman Rebel,* Sanger wrote " No God-No Masters," and referred to Christianity as "tyranny of mankind." In another book, *Women and the New Race,* she stated, "The most merciful thing a large family can do to one of its infant members is to kill it." Finally Sanger had to flee America under a forged name and passport after being indicted for publishing lewd and indecent materials.

Planned Parenthood is the leading provider of abortions in America. In spite of its misleading name this organization reportedly performed a staggering 2,425,508 abortions between 1977 and 1998.[7] Planned Parenthood received $176.5 million in government grants during 1998–99. The average abortion cost is $350, according to the Planned Parenthood web site. Based on this cost, Planned Parenthood's abortion income in 1998 was $58,774,800. The total estimated income generated by abortion in the U.S. for the year 1997 was $414,665,300.00.[8]

Knowing our hard-earned tax dollars are being used to kill innocent unborn babies should cause all Christians to fall on their faces before God, pray for revival, and do everything in their sphere of influence to stop this holocaust. Just for the record there are four hundred forty large, free-standing abortion chambers across America.[9] Other abortions take place in doctors' offices. When was the last time you prayed to stop the killing of unborn babies in your city or area?

Other subversive groups that have misleading names include National Organizations of Women (NOW), Americans United for Separation of Church and State, and the National Education Association (NEA).

5. In the 1970s the Supreme Court invented the so called "Lemon Test." This unworkable test requires government to interact with religion only if it has a secular purpose, does not endorse religion, or does not foster excessive governmental entanglement with religion. The "Lemon Test" was handed down in the case *Lemon v. Kurtzman.*[10] This convoluted test would push America further into a secular humanistic society.

6. As a whole, the preachers of America do not preach in context the truth of Romans 13:1–7. That truth is that government is an institution ordained of God. Therefore Christians need to be involved in and influence government. Proverbs 29:2 states "When the righteous are in authority the people rejoice: but when the wicked beareth rule, the people mourn." I pray the preachers and teachers of America will wake up and

preach the whole council of God. How can we have godly government such as our Founding Fathers gave us, if the congregations across America think government and politics are dirty words? The answer is, we won't until God's people put God-fearing men back in our government.

7. The last reason our foundations are being destroyed is because of executive orders. When a president creates a new law by executive order, our representative government is completely averted and any concept of checks and balances or separation of powers is no longer involved in the legislative process. Our U.S. Constitution grants no law-making power to the president or the executive branch of government. All legislative (law-making) power is granted to Congress according to Article 1, Section 8 of the U.S. Constitution.

The bottom line is this: Executive orders give the president the power to act as an unaccountable dictator. I wonder how many Americans know how Hitler converted Germany's republic into a Nazi dictatorship in just three months. It was through executive orders! Hitler also legalized abortion, euthanasia, and homosexuals in the military. He promoted environmental and animal rights, and passed thousands of laws and regulations that controlled every aspect of the German's lives. Finally, after Hitler had all the guns registered, he passed gun control laws to disarm the people. He then loaded the people in railcars, and took them to be killed in the Nazi death camps. Will Americans see the same deception happening in our nation before it's too late, or will she go down in history as the country who followed Germany's footsteps and lost everything?

I want to add, "martial law" and a declared "State of National Emergency" (real or manufactured) will only speed up this runaway governmental "freight train." Many of these E.O.s are "sitting in the wind" waiting for the right opportunity to be utilized.

It is clear to see from the court cases and other related information we have just discussed that there is an all-out attack on the God-ordained institutions of the family, government, and church. We desperately need a nationwide heaven-sent revival!

Chapter 5

We Ought to Obey God Rather Than Men (Acts 5:29)

It's time to ask another question. When does the Christian "obey God rather than men"? Recall Blackstone's law books stated, "If man's laws contradict God's laws in the Holy Scriptures, they are invalid." Therefore we as Christians must obey God's laws.

I want to give some examples from the Word of God where believers resisted ungodly laws, decrees, edicts, commandments and government.

The first example is found in Exodus 1:15–21. Pharaoh, the king of Egypt, commanded two midwives, Shiphrah and Puah, to kill the Hebrew baby boys when they were born. The midwives feared God and did not as the king commanded, but saved the boy babies. The midwives obeyed God's commandment, "Thou shall not kill," and disobeyed or resisted the king's commandment. Verses 20 and 21 go on to say, "Therefore God dealt well with the midwives . . . and because they feared God . . . he made them houses."

In Exodus 2, Moses' parents, Amram and Jochebed, disobeyed the king's law. This law charged all the Hebrews to cast their male babies into the river to drown (Exodus 1:22.) Moses' parents were not afraid of the king's commandment and hid him for three months (Hebrews 11:23). Amram and Jochebed had the fear of God, not the fear of man; therefore they obeyed God rather than men.

In Daniel 3, King Nebuchadnezzar made a decree or law. He commanded everyone to fall down and worship the golden image when they heard the music. Anyone refusing to worship the image would be cast into a fiery furnace. The three Hebrew children Shadrach, Meshach and Abednego refused or resisted the king's decree and would not bow down and worship the image. The Hebrew children obeyed God's law, "Thou shalt have no other gods before me or bow down to them," rather than the king's law. God honored their obedience by protecting then in the fiery furnace (Daniel 3:27).

There is another well-known story in the sixth chapter of the book of Daniel. King Darius established a royal statute and signed a decree that no one could pray to God or anyone else for thirty days except the king. The Bible states that Daniel "knew the decree was signed . . . but kneeled upon his knees three times a day, and prayed, and gave thanks before his God, as he did aforetime." Daniel obeyed God rather than the king. Because of Daniel's obedience, God delivered him out of the lions den (Daniel 6:21–22).

In the New Testament, in Acts 16:6–40 the apostle Paul and Silas were preaching the gospel to a demon-possessed woman and the people of the city Philippi. This was against Roman law according to verse twenty-one. The magistrates and rulers had Paul and Silas beaten, whipped, put in stock and chains, and thrown in prison. God delivered both of them through an earthquake and saved the prison guard and his family's souls, all because Paul and Silas obeyed God's law and not Roman law.

There are some pastors and teachers who believe a Christian owes "the powers that be" (government) absolute obedience. This is another myth and simply not biblical. Recall that the midwives, Moses' parents, the three Hebrew children, Daniel, and the apostle Paul did not obey the king or the laws that were contrary to God's laws. They "obeyed God rather than men."

Another passage of Scripture used out of context for absolute obedience to government is 1 Peter 2:13–14, "Submit yourselves to every ordinance of man for the Lord's sake: whether it be to the king, as supreme; Or unto governors, as unto them that are sent by him for the punishment of evildoers, and for the praise of them that do well."

Notice, we as Christians are to "submit to every ordinance of man for the Lord's sake. . . ." The Greek word used here for ordinance is a different word than is used in Romans 13:2. The Greek word for ordinance in Romans 13:2 literally means the institution of God. Here in 1 Peter 2:13 the Greek word for ordinance is *ktisis* and means formation. This simply means man "forms" the obedience or laws of God's "institution" or government according to God's principles, values, standards, and purposes. But we as Christians only submit to and obey those ordinances or laws that are in accordance with God's laws. Once again, "we ought to obey God rather than men."

The bottom line is this: When government steps out of its sphere of authority, it has no authority. The obedience due to government is only when that government is lawful according to the Word of God.

Exactly where do we as Christians draw the line in resisting ungodly government? How far do we go? When government comes after our children, when our property and guns are going to be confiscated, when they start telling us what to preach or not to preach at all?

I believe the Scriptures teach four basic methods of resistance to ungodly or tyrannical government and leaders.

The first method of resistance is verbal protest. Just a few biblical examples would include the three Hebrew children in Daniel chapter three. When they were commanded by the king to bow down and worship the golden image, the Hebrew children emphatically answered, ". . . We will not serve thy gods nor worship the golden image. . . ." In Acts 5:27–29 Peter and the apostles were commanded by the religious leaders and council not to teach in Jesus' name. They answered, "We ought to obey God rather than men." When we verbally resist ungodly government or leaders we might have to suffer the consequences in the form of a fine, jail sentence, or even execution. We as Christians cannot "serve two masters" (Luke 16:13). If we obey God as our only Master, we will always have "a conscience void of offence toward God, and toward men" (Acts 24:16). Verbally protesting unlawful or immoral actions of government and ecclesiastical leaders is how Protestants originally received this title. Are you a true Protestant?

The second method of resistance is legal action. Recall in Acts 25:11 that the apostle Paul appealed his case to Caesar because his civil rights had been violated. Paul used the Roman legal system to his advantage to further the "Great Commission" (Matthew 28:18–20).

If all avenues of verbal protest and legal action do not work, the third method of resistance is "flight." Jesus told his disciples in Matthew 10:23 ". . . When they persecute you in this city, flee ye into another. . . ."

In Matthew 2:13, Joseph and Mary were warned by an angel of the Lord that Herod was going to kill their baby, Jesus. In this dire situation Joseph arose in the middle of the night with his family and fled to Egypt. In 2 Corinthians 11:32–33, the apostle Paul fled and escaped from the governor of Damascus by going through a window in a basket and being lowered to the ground.

Many of the martyrs we discussed earlier fled to other cities and countries. The Pilgrims fled from England because of government and ecclesiastical tyranny.

The fourth method of resistance is "force in self-defense." This method is the last recourse to be used only after we have exhausted the other three methods in order. There are Christians who would disagree with this method of "force in self-defense." Let's review the Scripture.

The Old Testament contains many examples of the children of Israel using force to defend themselves. One of the best examples is found in Nehemiah 4. Sanballat and Tobiah, along with the Ammonites and Arabians, had conspired to come and fight against Jerusalem. Nehemiah, the governor, prepared the Jews to fight against their adversaries. He was not going to allow these enemies to stop or destroy the work of God. Nehemiah did so by setting the people around and on the wall they were rebuilding with their swords, spears, and bows.

In verse fourteen Nehemiah stated, "Be not ye afraid of them: remember the Lord . . . and fight for your brethren, your sons, and your daughters, your wives, and your houses." The Hebrew word for fight used in this passage is *lacham* which means to battle or make war. We can see from this passage a just battle or war is legitimate when an adversary threatens your family, your Christian friends, or your house and property.

Nehemiah continues speaking in verses sixteen through eighteen. ". . . Half of my servants wrought in the work, and the other half of them held both the spears, the shields, and the bows, and the habergeons . . . They which builded on the wall . . . held a weapon . . . every one had his sword girded by his side, and so builded. . . ." Notice "every one had his sword girded by his side." Speaking of swords, in Luke 22:36 Jesus told His disciples at the conclusion of the Last Supper, ". . .He that hath no sword let him sell his garment and buy one."

Once again the final method of "force in self-defense" is used only after the other methods of resistance have been exhausted. "Force in self-defense" may be used to defend the work of God, but not to advance the work of God. We as Christians are not conquistadors. We do not take our swords and guns and put them to the heads of people and say, "Become a Christian and get baptized or its off with your head."

Our Founding Fathers used "force in self-defense." Do you realize the only reason we enjoy all the freedoms, liberties, and privileges that we do in American is because our Founding Fathers resisted the king of Great Britain? Our nation's number one document, the Declaration of Independence states the reasons our Founding Fathers resisted and separated themselves from Great Britain. In the Declaration of Independence are twenty-seven usurpations or abuses committed by the king of Great Britain against the people of the thirteen colonies.

The Founding Fathers believed they had certain God-given, unalienable rights and one of them was resisting or separating themselves from ungodly, tyrannical oppressive government. The Declaration of Independence states, "In every stage of these oppressions we have Petitioned for Redress in the most humble terms. Our repeated petitions have been answered only by repeated injury. A prince, whose character is thus marked by every act which may define a Tyrant, is unfit to be the ruler of a free people."

The Declaration of Independence also states:

> We therefore the Representatives of the United States of America, in General Congress, Assembled, appealing to the Supreme Judge of the world for the rectitude of our intentions . . . declare . . . these United Colonies . . . to be Free and Independent States . . . and for the support of this Declaration, with a firm reliance on the protection of Divine Providence we mutually pledge to each other our Lives, our Fortunes, and our Sacred honor.

It is clear to see the Declaration of Independence followed the biblical methods of resistance for "obeying God rather than men." It is also clear to see the Declaration of Independence was not a declaration of rebellion, but rather a declaration of dependence on God and resistance to ungodly tyrannical government. Benjamin Franklin stated, "Rebellion to tyrants is obedience to God" and wanted to use this motto for the seal of the new United States.[1]

Chapter 6

The "Black Regiment"
of American Preachers

Very few Christians realize today we would not have a Declaration of Independence if it were not for the "Black Regiment." This is the name King George gave the preachers of America. He called them the "Black Regiment" because of the black clerical robes they wore while preaching. King George feared these preachers more than any other elements of society.[1]

The reason they were feared was because these colonial preachers opposed the "Divine Right of Kings"[2] and refused to take a "state license" from the British government. These preachers would thunder from the pulpits, "No king but King Jesus."[3]

There were approximately thirty-two hundred Christian churches in the American colonies in 1775.[4] These large numbers were a direct result of the "Great Awakening" and the powerful preaching of Jonathan Edwards and George Whitfield during the 1730s to 1750s.

The "Black Regiment" preachers were branded by the king of England as "dissenters" and "non-conformists."[5] Many of these unlicensed preachers were thrown into prison, beaten, whipped, and all of their possessions seized. The greatest defender of the "dissenter" preachers was Founding Father Patrick Henry. Read carefully the following incident.

In March of 1775, Patrick Henry was riding through the small town of Culpepper, Virginia. As he rode into the town square, he was completely shocked by what he witnessed. There, in the middle of the town square, was a man tied to a whipping post, his back laid bare, his bones exposed. He had been scourged mercilessly with whips laced with metal. When they stopped beating him, Patrick Henry could plainly see the bones of his rib cage. He turned to ask someone in the crowd, "What has the man done to deserve such a beating as this?" The reply given him was that the man being scourged was a minister. He was one of twelve ministers locked in jail because they refused to take the king's license to preach the gospel. The governor was under orders from King George to compel all preachers to take the license. While being tried, without the benefit of a jury, the minister stated, "I will never submit to taking your license. I am controlled by the Holy Spirit, and authorized by God Almighty, and will not allow you to control me by a license, no matter what you may do to me." Three days later, he was scourged to death.

This was the incident that sparked Patrick Henry to write the famous words, which later became the rallying cry of the American Revolution, "Is life so dear, or peace so sweet, as to purchase the price of chains and slavery? Forbid it, Almighty God! I know not what course others may take, but as for me, give me liberty, or give me death."[6] As a common-law lawyer, Patrick Henry would win the release of many a preacher from prison. He would also pay their fines or post bail anonymously.

Because of the "Black Regiment," the king of Great Britain made the pastors and churches of the thirteen colonies a primary military target. The reason being, many preachers could enlist more men into the military than George Washington himself. Many of the church buildings served as militia headquarters, armories, and hospitals. The churches also formed the famous "Minutemen" and the deacons of the church would be responsible for drilling them. Later they would go into the church for "artillery sermons."[7] These sermons addressed topics such as "a defensive war in a just cause is sinless." The most historic band of Minutemen was led by Deacon Parker under the Reverend Jonas Clark in Lexington, Massachusetts. In 1775 this is where the "shot heard round the world" was fired.

One of the most inspirational and stirring stories of preachers leading their congregations into battle is that of the Reverend John Muhlenberg.[8] He was a Lutheran pastor in Woodstock, Virginia. Reverend Muhlenberg's congregation had already sent supplies to their brethren in Boston. This was not enough, so he preached a message the following Sunday from Ecclesiastes 3:1–8: "To every thing there is a season, and a time to every purpose under the heavens: a time to be born, and a time to die; . . . a time to weep, and a time to laugh; . . . a time of war, and a time of peace."

At the end of his sermon, Reverend Muhlenberg raised his voice and exclaimed ". . . And there is a time to fight, and that time has now come." Sound the drums! He then proceeded to take off his black clerical robe to reveal the uniform of a Virginia colonel. Putting on his three-cornered colonel's hat, he grabbed his musket from behind the pulpit, raised it high in the air and quoted Nehemiah 4:14, "Be not ye afraid of them; remember the Lord, which is great and terrible, and fight for your brethren, your sons, and your daughters, your wives, and your houses." Reverend Muhlenberg enlisted all the able-bodied men in his congregation and hundreds more. He was soon promoted to Rev. Major General Muhlenberg. This is the reason the king of Great Britain targeted the pastors and churches. Therefore, the British commanders were given specific orders to kill pastors and chaplains and to burn their homes, churches, and libraries.

Just one of many heart-wrenching examples would include the Reverend James Caldwell of Springfield, New Jersey. While Rev. Caldwell was away, the British army shot and killed his wife. They also set the house on fire with his nine children in it. Fortunately the servant girl was able to get all of the children out alive. She got word to Rev. Caldwell, who rode all night and then buried his wife. Later the British army returned. The Patriots took cover behind the church but ran out of paper wadding used to hold the powder and ball in place in their muskets. Rev. Caldwell ran into his church, grabbed all the Watts hymnals he could carry, tore out the pages of the hymnals and gave them to the men, shouting "Put Watts into 'em boys! Give 'em Watts!"[9]

Another tactic the king of Great Britain and the British army used was the desecration of churches. The "Old South Church" in Boston was turned into a riding academy for the British army. The pulpit and pews were taken out and burned for fuel.[10] The Presbyterian church at Newtown Long Island was used as a prison by the British after sawing off its steeple, and churches in New York City were also made into prisons. At least fifty churches throughout the thirteen colonies were totally destroyed and dozens more damaged.[11]

Now you know why we have a president instead of a king in America. Our Founding Fathers realized the natural tendency of man's heart is to do wrong. This concept is found in Jeremiah 17:9, "The heart is deceitful above all things, and desperately wicked: who can know it?" Because man's heart is deceitful and power-hungry, our Founding Fathers did not want the power of a nation to rest in one official such as a king. If the king became corrupt, the whole nation would suffer. If the power could be separated and balanced, all of the government would not become corrupt at the same time.

The concept used by our Founding Fathers to separate our governmental power into three branches is found in Isaiah 33:22, "For the Lord is our judge, the Lord is our lawgiver, the Lord is our king, he will save us." Our judicial branch of government was formed from the attribute of God being our Judge. Our legislative branch of government was formed from the attribute of God being our Lawgiver. Our executive branch of government was formed from the attribute of God being our King. This last attribute of God being our King is where the Founding Fathers derived the motto "No king but King Jesus."

Chapter 7

Biblical Duties and Responsibilities
of Rulers (Romans 13:3-4)

If we look again at the first verse of Romans 13, it reads: "Let every soul be subject unto the higher powers . . . the powers that be are ordained of God." This includes kings, presidents, and their cabinet, Supreme Court justices, congressmen, lawyers, and all state, federal, and local government positions. These government officials are not above the law. Every soul is to be subject or submitted to God's laws. As Christians, we cannot always submit to the government official, if his laws contradict God's laws, but we must have respect and submit to the office itself that is ordained of God. Speaking of government officials, let's move on to verses three and four of Romans 13.

> For rulers are not a terror to good works, but to the evil. Wilt thou then not be afraid of the power? do that which is good, and thou shalt have praise of the same: For he is the minister of God to thee for good. But if thou do that which is evil, be afraid; for he beareth not the sword in vain: for he is the minister of God, a revenger to execute wrath upon him that doeth evil.

These inspired verses give us the duties and responsibilities of rulers and government officials. The first word we want to define from verse three is ruler. To properly understand the biblical duty of a ruler we need to look at the qualifications of a ruler. Exodus 18:21 states: "Moreover thou shalt provide out of all the people able men, such as fear God, men of truth, hating covetousness; and place such over them, to be rulers of thousands, and rulers of hundreds, rulers of fifties, and rulers of tens."

Notice the four qualifications for rulers: to be able, to fear God, to be truthful, and to hate covetousness. If a ruler does not have the fear of God he will be a man-pleaser and compromise biblical absolutes. A ruler must study and know truth from the Bible. John 17:17 states, ". . . Thy word is truth." A ruler must hate covetousness—he cannot serve two masters—he will hate the one, and love the other (Luke 16:13).

Second Samuel 23:3 states, "The God of Israel said . . . He that ruleth over men must be just, ruling in the fear of God." A ruler must be just. This is accomplished by using God's absolute standard of justice found in the Word of God. Once again, a ruler must rule in the fear of God and not the fear of man. He must never be swayed by public opinion or a bribe.

In verse four of Romans 13 a ruler is called the "minister of God" two times. The Greek word for minister is *diakonia* and means a waiter or servant at tables, a Christian teacher, or technically a deacon. Therefore from the local town mayor to the president of the United States is as much a minister of God as the local pastor, but in a different way.

If we look into the history of rulers, we will find God originally forbade Israel to have a king. In 1 Samuel 8, Israel wanted a king to judge them so they could be like all the other nations. Samuel warned the children of Israel what manner of king would rule over them. But they said, "We will have a king over us."

The king would take their sons and daughters and make them servants. Their sons would serve the king by fighting in his army. The king would also take a tenth of their sheep, vineyards, and seeds.

Other rules for kings of Israel are found in Deuteronomy 17. Verse fifteen states the king must be chosen by God, be from among the brethren, and not a stranger or a foreigner. In other words the king must be a believer in Jehovah God.

Verse sixteen states that he shall not multiply horses to himself. God wanted the king and the people to rely and trust Him for their defense and not "chariots and horses" (Psalm 20:7). Recall, war machinery is always defensive, not offensive. If American has ten million nuclear warheads and God is not with us, we will lose the battle.

Verse seventeen states that he shall not multiply wives to himself. Rulers must be moral. A ruler or government official that will lie and cheat on his wife, will lie and cheat on the people. A government official that could care less about his own family will not care for my wife and children. If a government official is perverted, he will not think twice about perverting my children. Once again, rulers must be moral!

Verse seventeen also states that a ruler shall not greatly multiply silver and gold. We need to make sure our government officials are not involved in government just for the money.

Verse eighteen states that the king is to write a copy of the law in a book. This means he is to have his own personal copy of the Word of God which contains the laws of God.

Verse nineteen states that the king or government official is to read therein all the days of his life. This is so he will have wisdom and the fear of God and not the fear of man. The king is also to keep all the words of God's law. Notice that the king (or Supreme Court judges) could not make their own laws, but must secure God's laws.

Verse twenty states that he cannot let his heart be lifted up above his brethren. The ruler cannot be proud or power-hungry.

Now that we have researched and discussed the qualifications of a ruler, let's research how the rulers were chosen.

Acts 14:23 states: "And when they had ordained them elders in every church, and had prayed with fasting, they commended them to the Lord, on whom they believed." The Greek word for ordained in this verse is *cheirotoneo* and means to be a voter (by raising the hand). This was the method used by the apostles to elect their leaders in the original church.

The godly Pilgrims used this biblical precedent of the hand-vote in their church government according to the marginal notes in the Geneva Bible. Soon afterward, the Pilgrims simply transferred the use of the hand-vote from their church government over to their civil government.

According to the "Mayflower Compact," the Pilgrims not only came to America for the "advancement of the Christian faith" but to form a "civil body politic." The "Mayflower Compact" also stated this civil body politic would use just laws, ordinances, acts, constitutions, and offices to preserve and further the advancement of the Christian faith.

By 1624 the Pilgrims had annual elections of office for a governor and seven assistants.[1] The hand-vote was used in the elections. In 1633, the Pilgrims used an "election sermon"[2] before the actual voting took place. Today, most government officials, American citizens, and Christians have never heard of an "election sermon." Let me explain how it worked. The governor and elected officials would appoint local pastors to preach sermons on the day of election. These sermons would deal with the biblical qualifications and responsibilities of public officials and citizens. The "election sermon" was printed and every representative and official had a copy for himself. The "election sermon" would continue to be used for over two hundred fifty years.[3] Listen to how a foreigner from Great Britain by the name of Edward Kendall described an election day in America.

> . . . The procession of the governor [of Connecticut] was made to a . . . church . . . and was composed of lieutenant, governor, assistants, high-sheriffs, and members of the lower house assembly. The pulpit . . . was filled by . . . four clergymen. . . . One of these opened the service with a prayer, another delivered a sermon, a third made a concluding prayer, and a fourth pronounced a benediction. Several hymns were sung. . . . The total number of singers was between forty and fifty. . . . The sermon . . . touched upon matters of government. . . .[4]

This election sermon in Connecticut was given in 1807, two decades after the U.S. Constitution was drafted. This election sermon was also delivered in a church, with prayer, and the singing of hymns. There is no evidence of the myth of "separation of church and state" which would be used today to forbid this kind of an election day.

Four large books with over five thousand pages entitled *Political Sermons and Writing During the Founding Era*[5] are filled with election sermons from 1730 to 1805. Here are a few of the titles. "Civil Magistrates Must Be Just, Ruling in the Fear of God"[6] taken from 2 Samuel 23:3. This election sermon was preached by Reverend Charles Chauncy D.D. of the First Church in Boston to the House of Representatives in Massachusetts. The sermon is thirty-six pages in length and twenty-six Bible verses are used.

An "election sermon" preached by the Reverend Samuel West was entitled "On the Right to Rebel Against Governors."[7] Reverend West was another revered and highly influential clergyman in Dartmouth, Massachusetts. This election sermon is taken from Titus 3:1 is thirty-eight pages long, and was also preached to the House of Representatives in Massachusetts.

Remember now, after the election sermon was preached the people would vote. Amazingly the election sermons were used for two and one-half centuries.

Another powerful election sermon preached by the Reverend Peter Powers was entitled "Jesus Christ, the True King and Head of Government" (Document B) based on Matthew 28:18. The General Assembly of Vermont asked Reverend Powers to address them on March 12, 1778, the first day of their election in Windsor, Vermont. Powers declared:

> We have renounced the tyrant of Britain and declaimed loudly against monarchical power and have set up a free people. We own no other prince or sovereign but the Prince of Heaven, the great Sovereign of the Universe. To Him we swear allegiance and promise, through His abundant grace, to keep His laws.[8]

The General Assembly of Vermont ordered that address to be printed and distributed among the people.

Before we go on, I must document some of the results and fruits from the early election sermons.

On May 31, 1638, the famous Puritan minister Thomas Hooker preached a sermon of wonderful power at the opening session of the General Court in Hartford, Connecticut.[9] The sermon text was taken from Deuteronomy 1:13 and was preached from the pulpit of the First Church in Hartford. It was the earliest known suggestion of fundamental law.

Eight months later, America's first constitution, called the "Fundamental Orders of Connecticut,"[10] was penned by Roger Ludlow after hearing this sermon. From this time on, Connecticut became known as "The Constitution State" and all the license plates still have the same title on them today. The committee framing the orders (laws) was charged to make the laws "as near the law of God as they can be."[11]

This first constitution of Connecticut was adopted on January 14, 1639, by all the freemen of the three towns of Hartford. It was the first written constitution known in history that created a government. The preamble stated:

Forasmuch as it has pleased the Almighty God by the wise disposition of
His divine providence so to order and dispose of things that we the inhabitants and residents of Windsor, Hartford and Wethersfield and now cohabiting and dwelling in and upon the River Connecticut and the lands thereunto adjoining; and well knowing when a people are gathered together the
Word of God requires, that to maintain the peace and union of such a people,
there should be an orderly and decent government established according to
God, to order and dispose of the affairs of all the people at all seasons as
occasion shall require; do therefore associate and conjoin ourselves to be as
one public State or Commonwealth, and do, for ourselves and our successors and such as shall be adjoined to us at any time hereafter, enter into
combination and Confederation together, to maintain and preserve the liberty and purity of the Gospel of our Lord Jesus which we now profess. . .
.Which, according to the truth of the said Gospel, is now practiced amongst
us; as also, in our civil affairs to be guided and governed according to such
laws, rules, orders, and decrees.[12]

Notice, America's first constitution was established according to God, main-
taining and preserving the gospel of our Lord Jesus Christ, and that all civil
affairs would be guided and governed by such laws, rules, orders, and decrees. According to the great historian John Fiske speaking in 1889 the government of the United States today is more in the lineal descent to that of
Connecticut than to any of the other colonies.[13]

America's first constitution was so successful and revolutionary that
Massachusetts was inspired to adopt a "Body of Liberties" in 1641. These
ninety-eight liberties were a code of laws taken from the Word of God by the
Reverend Nathaniel Ward of Ipswich. A few of those liberties included the
right to life, the right to trial by jury, the right to own private property and
no taxation without representation. The "Body of Liberties" also contained
laws for capitol crimes.[14] Does all of this sound familiar? It should! These
liberties, rights, and laws led directly to the ideas and concepts used and
found in the Declaration of Independence, U.S. Constitution, and Bill of
Rights. These godly Pilgrims and Puritans studied the Bible, and found it
prescribed the best political and economic systems.

The "Body of Liberties" and the first written constitution in America, along with other similar documents, establish that Christianity was the prominent influence of early civil government in the New World.

Still another "political sermon" I want to tell you about from one of the four books we just discussed will surprise and inspire every God-fearing American. Let me set the stage for this sermon by asking a few questions. What was the largest church in America from 1800 during President Thomas Jefferson's administration and up until the Civil War? Where did the largest church in America meet?

The nation's largest church during these fifty-some years met in the most visible public building in America, the U.S. Capitol.[15] That's correct! The U.S. Capitol. The Sixth Congress authorized the Capitol building to be used as a church building on December 4, 1800.[16] All Christian denominations were included in the invitation to preach. Thousands joined in the House of Representatives each Sunday to worship God, including President Thomas Jefferson, cabinet members, senators, and the general public. On Christmas Day December 25, 1804, a sermon was delivered before both Houses of Congress in the Capitol building. The sermon was entitled "On the Second Coming of Christ and on the Last Judgment" by the Reverend John Hargrove.[17] Can you imagine that? I personally would not agree with all of the teachings from this sermon, but the fact remains that our U.S. Capitol building was used as a church building for over half a century.

This practice, approved by Congress, repudiates all of today's erroneous doctrines of "separation of church and state," which claims our Founding Fathers would never approve of religious activities in official public buildings.

Our Founding Fathers used biblical principles and values for selecting rulers. Listen to just a few of the strong statements from our Founding Fathers, about whom we should elect for our rulers.

John Jay, the first Supreme Court Justice of the United States Supreme Court, president of the American Bible Society, and president of the Westchester Bible Society, stated: "Providence has given to our people the choice of their rulers, and it is the duty, as well as the privilege and interest of our Christian nation to select and prefer Christians for their rulers."[18] Notice John Jay called America a Christian nation and said we should elect Christians for our rulers. When was the last time you heard a Supreme Court

Justice say that? John Jay was once asked if it were permissible for a Christian to vote for an ungodly candidate. He said "no" and quoted 2 Chronicles 19:2 ". . . Shouldest thou help the ungodly? . . . therefore is wrath upon thee from before the Lord."[19]

Founding Father Noah Webster gives us more insight on the process of choosing rulers.

> In selecting men for office, let principle be your guide . . . look to his character. . . . It is alleged by men of loose principles, or defective views of the subject, that religion and morality are not necessary or important qualifications for public station. . . . Let the wise counsel of Jethro (Exodus 18:21) . . . be your guide. Choose ye out from among you able men, such as fear God, men of truth and hating covetousness and set them to rule over you. . . . When a citizen gives his suffrage [vote] to a man of known immorality, he abuses this trust [civil responsibility], he sacrifices not only his own interest, but that of his neighbor, he betrays the interest of this country.[20]

Noah Webster made it clear that if moral and godly men are not selected for office, it would certainly result in government corruption.

When an individual became elected, prior to taking his position and performing his duties, he first had to take an oath of office. Let's review some of the oaths for holding public office.

The Pennsylvania state constitution of 1776 stated:

> I do believe in one God, the creator and governor of the universe, the rewarder of the good and a punisher of the wicked and I do acknowledge the Holy Scriptures of the Old and New Testament to be given by divine inspiration.

Delaware's constitution of 1776 stated:

> I do profess faith in God the Father and in Jesus Christ, his only Son and in the Holy Ghost, one God, blessed forevermore, and I do acknowledge the Holy Scriptures of the Old and New Testament to be given by divine inspiration.[21]

Maryland's Constitution of 1864 which was almost three quarters of a century after the ratification of the U.S. Constitution stated:

A declaration of belief in the Christian religion, or of the existence of God, and in a future state of rewards and punishments.[22]

Notice the candidate was required to believe in the "Trinity," consisting of the Father, the Son, and Holy Ghost, divine inspiration of all the Holy Scriptures and a future state of rewards in Heaven and punishment in Hell. Remember, these requirements were not for seminary but requirements to be a politician. It is clear to see a person was selected not because they were a good politician, but because they were a good Christian politician.

Another important point to be made is how one vote can change the course of a nation. Here are a few examples: By one vote America chose the English language over the German language in 1775. By one vote Founding Father Caesar Rodney broke the Delaware deadlock and gave America independence in 1776. By one vote Adolf Hitler won leadership of the German Nazi party in 1923. And most recently, George W. Bush won the 2000 presidential election by a few hundred votes, giving him the most electoral college votes.

We can see from these examples how absolutely critical it is for all Christians to become informed and vote in all of their local, state, and federal elections.

Do you vote in all elections? Are you registered to vote? If not, why not? If you don't vote, someone else's vote is going to make a decision for you. Think about that!

We need to eliminate the popular myth of today that Christians should not influence or be involved in politics. We have been told politics are dirty or unspiritual. The only reason politics have become dirty and unspiritual as a whole, is because the majority of Christians have abandoned this God-ordained biblical institution.

Proverbs, the book of wisdom, gives the reason why much of our government, our laws, and our courts are corrupt. Proverbs 29:2 states, "When the righteous are in authority, the people rejoice: but when the wicked beareth rule, the people mourn." Let me ask you a question concerning this verse.

When you watch the news on TV or read the daily newspaper, do you rejoice or mourn? Most of the time we as Christians mourn. The main reason for this is because we have allowed the wicked or ungodly to be put in office and now they are ruling over us. May I please point out to you, it is not possible to elect Christians to rule over us if true Christians are not running for office. Proverbs 29:12 states, "If a ruler hearken to lies, all his servants are wicked." This means an ungodly ruler will have and appoint wicked aides to his staff. This is exactly what happened in much of the Clinton administration.

More Christians need to get involved in their local, state, and federal government because it is our Christian responsibility. If we do not get involved, our nation is only going to get worse. Proverbs 14:34 states, "Righteousness exalteth a nation: but sin is a reproach to any people." Psalm 9:17 states, "The wicked shall be turned into hell, and all the nations that forget God." We as Christians not only have the responsibility of electing godly officials but to pray for them after they are in office. First Timothy 2:1–2 states, "I exhort therefore, that, first of all, supplications, prayers, intercessions, and giving of thanks, be made for all men; For kings, and for all that are in authority; that we may lead a quiet and peaceful life in all godliness and honesty."

May I encourage you to pray daily for our president and his cabinet, Congress, Supreme Court justices, governors, and all federal, state, and local officials including your town mayor, judges, and lawyers, city council members, county commissioners, the local school board, principals, teachers, and law enforcement officers.

One of the reasons we have so much violence, ungodliness, and dishonesty in America is because we as Christians have not prayed for our rulers. If you have not prayed for your government officials, please do so on a daily basis, starting today. Also remember to thank God for the good Christian officials we do have in our government.

Verses three and four of 1 Timothy 2 tell us that praying for our government officials ". . . is good and acceptable in the sight of God our Savior; who will have all men to be saved, and to come unto the knowledge of the truth." We also need to pray for the salvation of all government officials in America and around the world who do not know Jesus Christ as Savior and Lord.

Chapter 8

Biblical Functions of Government
(Romans 13:3 & 1 Peter 2:14)

Now that we have researched the biblical qualifications for rulers and the godly heritage of our electoral process, we will research the purpose or function of the God-ordained institution of government.

Recall, Romans 13:3 gives two basic functions of government. The first function is "not to be a terror to good works." This means government is not to put "fear" into those people and organizations that are doing good works. On the contrary government is to promote and protect good works. Some examples would be the spreading of the gospel, the preaching of the whole council of God, protecting the sanctity of life, upholding all moral absolutes, principles, and values in the Word of God. Our republican government did promote and protect "good works" from its beginning until a few decades ago. When the government performs this function of promoting and protecting "good works," then "we the people" can "lead a quiet and peaceable life in all godliness and honesty."

The second basic function of government found in verse three is for government to be a "terror to the evil." In other words, government is to punish evildoers and criminals. First Peter 2:14 also states that government is to ". . . punish the evildoers. . . ."

Verse four of Romans 13 tells us how government is to punish evildoers. ". . . But if thou do that which is evil, be afraid; for he [government] beareth not the sword in vain: for he [government] is the minister of God, a revenger to execute wrath upon him that doeth evil."

According to this verse God has given government power to enforce itself and its laws. Therefore this verse unquestionably provides New Testament justification for capital punishment. This "Divine directive" was established after the worldwide flood in Noah's day in Genesis 9:6 stating, "Whoso sheddeth man's blood, by man shall his blood be shed. . . ." This verse was not given as part of the Mosaic law. These words were revealed before there ever was an Israelite nation. They are as binding today as God's instructions for marriage in Genesis 2:24.

The death penalty or capital punishment is biblical and not barbaric, as some would say. Few issues are more emotion-charged than this one. There are those who think it is absolutely un-Christian and barbaric to execute a convicted murderer.

The word "sword" used in verse four of Romans 13 would symbolize today's use of the electric chair or lethal injection for capitol punishment. The sword is an instrument of death and indicates execution. The apostle Paul believed in the death penalty and that government is a "revenger to execute wrath on evildoers" when he answered Festus in Acts 25:11 stating, "For if I be an offender, or have committed any thing worthy of death, I refuse not to die."

The sixth commandment states, "Thou shall not kill" (Exodus 20:13). Yes, the Bible says there is a prohibition against killing, but what kind of killing—mosquitoes on a hot muggy day? chickens at the slaughter house?— or is there some other meaning. The congregation of Israel was instructed by God to "kill" the Passover lamb (Exodus 12:21). All killing, therefore, can't be wrong.

The Hebrew word used for kill in this verse is *ratsach* and means to murder or a (man) slayer. Therefore this commandment "Thou shall not kill" in context is not prohibiting all killing, but is prohibiting the unlawful taking of human life, i.e. "murder."

The Greek word for revenger in verse four of Romans 13 is *ekdikos* and means a "punisher who carries out justice." Therefore, it is not wrong for the man (minister of God) who pulls the switch for the evil murderer in the electric chair or gives the lethal injection. He is acting as a "revenger of God to execute wrath."

Another purpose of execution is to be a deterrent. If a man knows he will be put to death for killing a person, he will think twice. On the other hand, if a man thinks he can get off the hook by a slick lawyer or liberal judge, he will probably commit the crime. I want to add that government was never ordained or commanded by God to be a provider for welfare for unwed or divorced mothers, elderly folks, or widows. This kind of welfare is to be provided by the church and individual families according to 1 Timothy 5:4–9. Neither was government ordained to provide for an education or health care. These unconstitutional and unscriptural polices are helping to destroy and bankrupt America.

Our American government fulfilled the two basic biblical functions of promoting and protecting good works and punishing evildoers for approximately one hundred and fifty years, or until the 1960s.

As stated earlier, our Christian foundations started to be destroyed by instituting the "case law methods" in our universities. Today our American courts now use law dictionaries instead of law books like *Blackstone's Commentaries* with Bible verses.

In today's law dictionaries you will find no Bible verses for absolute truth and morals, no references to God, or any indication America was founded as a Christian nation. Here is what you will find. The definition of law from one dictionary states:

> Our laws are derived from . . . divine or moral laws and human experience, as [each] . . . has been evolved by human intellect influenced by the virtues of the ages. Human laws must therefore of necessity continually change as human experience shall prove the necessity of new laws . . . or as public conscience shall change, thus viewing matters from a different moral viewpoint.[1]

Did you catch the radical flip-flop and reversal of "change . . . to new laws . . . as public conscience shall change . . . from a different moral viewpoint"? This is nothing more than secular humanism in the extreme from the pit of hell. This definition of law is a million miles removed from our original law books. Recall Blackstone's law books stated ". . . No human law should be allowed to contradict these . . . [Holy Scriptures]." Other well-known law dictionaries give about the same secular humanistic definitions.

If our present day law dictionaries do not give the proper definition for law as intended by our Founding Fathers, how could you trust the law dictionary for other words?

In the last few decades, America has gone from being a republic to an oligarchy, which is the rule of an elite few. These elite few are basically the nine Supreme Court Justices. Our government, through the courts, soon started getting involved in many unconstitutional, unscriptural, illegal, and "special" rights, including abortion, homosexuality, euthanasia, illegal aliens, radical feminism, and radical environmentalism.

Our number one document, the Declaration of Independence, states the purpose of our government is "to secure our God-given unalienable rights," not to make rights. Sadly, today many of our courts from the top to the bottom are making rights instead of securing our rights as originally intended by our Founding Fathers. With the stroke of a pen, the courts, judges, and lawyers can make or change any law or ruling they choose.

Chapter 9

The New World Order

So far we have researched, documented, and discussed many different aspects of our government, laws and courts. It is clear to see our government as a whole is quickly going in the direction of corruption when compared with its original Christian foundations, principles, and values.

It's time to ask ourselves a very sobering question. Where is government ultimately taking us? According to the Word of God we are heading "smack dab" into a world government ruled by a wicked world dictator. Revelation 13:7 states, ". . . Power was given him over all kindreds, and tongues, and nations."

The person referred to in this passage has been called the Antichrist by Christians. This Antichrist, or world dictator, will have power over all kindreds, which means races, including red, yellow, black, and white, all tongues meaning every language, and all nations. The word power used in this verse and also verses four, five, and twelve means "force, magistrate, and superhuman." In other words, this world magistrate or dictator will be superhuman or Satan-possessed and will use force to rule the earth.

The movers and shakers promoting and establishing world government have named it the New World Order.[1] Most of us became familiar with the phrase "New World Order" in the eighties. The New World Order is really not new. Its beginning goes back thousands of years to the Tower of Babel, described in Genesis 10–11. This is when Nimrod "began to be a mighty one in the earth . . . and the beginning of his kingdom was Babel." The literal Hebrew definition for these words means, "the first powerful tyrant to unify by force and become famous." In addition, all people were of one language, one speech, and said, "Let us make us a name." This first attempt of the New World Order failed because of God's divine intervention. Since that time, many more attempts have been made, but they also ended in failure.

Today, in the new millennium, the New World Order, or global coalition, is alive and well, as we shall soon find out.

Even the FBI has a thirty-two page report entitled "Project Megiddo." It contains a section about the "New World Order Conspiracy Theory." Some of the warnings found in "Project Megiddo" are timely and well taken, but the report paints all Christians as "extremists." The report defines an extremist as one who believes in the end of the world and the Second Coming of Christ.

Our former president, George H. Bush, used the phrase "New World Order" over two hundred times during his administration.[2] President Bush defined the details of the New World Order in a speech at the National Religious Broadcasters Convention in Washington, D.C. To an audience of about four thousand people, he implied: "You know what is going to solve all our problems? There is something called the New World Order. When this comes in, it's going to bring peace as we have never seen. We are going to be able to lay down all our weapons. The New World Order is the solution to all our problems."[3]

If only President Bush had known! The peace of the New World Order will be a false peace and a living nightmare come true. First Thessalonians 5:3 states: "For when they shall say, Peace and safety; then sudden destruction cometh upon them, as travail upon a woman with child; and they shall not escape."

In the mid-nineties, hundreds of world leaders and thousands of businessmen would unite in San Francisco, California, to promote the New World Order. Who do you think was heading up this big meeting? An article, dated February 3, 1995, from one of California's largest newspapers, the *San Francisco Chronicle*, states:

> Former Soviet President Mikhail Gorbachev has asked hundreds of world leaders and thousands of business people to join him in San Francisco next autumn to discuss the state of the world. The idea behind the forum, from September 27 to October 1, is to. . . look at fundamental priorities and values that the world should embrace. Hopes for a new world order . . . have dimmed, "and there is a yearning for new directions," said former Senator Alan Cranston, D-California, chairman of the Gorbachev Foundation, U.S.A.

Amazingly, Mikhail Gorbachev has been holding "State of the World Forums" in our own backyard since 1995. Remember now, "the idea behind the forum is to look at fundamental priorities and values which the world should embrace." There was a list of forty-two presentations recorded at the 1995 Forum.[4] You will be shocked at the similarities between the sugarcoated titles and the four world systems of Revelation 13: "Emerging Global Political and Security Trends," "Global Security," "Seeking Genuine Disarmament," "The Global Crisis of Spirit and the Search for Meaning," "The New Science of the Sacred," and "Technology and Labor in the Global Economy." The other thirty-eight presentations revolve around the same basic themes.

The State of the World Forum included an array of co-chairmen, namely former president George H. Bush, former British prime minister Margaret Thatcher, Nobel Peace Prize winner Archbishop Desmond Tutu, and cable TV magnate Ted Turner. The forum was also a "coming-out party" for New Age elitists. Among those present were John Denver, Shirley MacLaine, Carl Sagan, Barbara Marx Hubbard, Maurice Strong, Robert Muller, and Michael Murphy, just to name a few. The annual "State of the World Forum" meetings are being held by the Gorbachev Foundation U.S.A. at the Presidio in San Francisco. The Presidio, at one time, was one of America's most hallowed U.S. military bases, built to defend America. Now it is being used by Mikhail Gorbachev to promote the blueprint for the New World Order—a global *perestroika*—right in our own backyard. How sad!

For more information on the "State of the World Forums," access their website at *www.worldforum.org.*

Finally, this article from the *San Francisco Chronicle* stated that Mikhail Gorbachev wanted to create an "informal brain trust," for a so-called Earth Charter, described as an "environmental bill of rights." Both the "informal brain trust" and Earth Charter are now realities through his special, powerful, and international organization, Green Cross Family. Gorbachev's website for Green Cross Family opens with the following words: "We need a new system of values, a system of the organic unity between mankind and nature and the ethic of global responsibility." This statement has become Gorbachev's campaign slogan. This radical, all-encompassing, planetary document called The Earth Charter is a bill of rights for the planet. If implemented, it would give the environment far greater rights than "we the people." Humanity would literally become a slave to the earth and to the global regime who would enforce these mandates.

Gorbachev described his new Earth Charter as "a new set of rules to guide humanity."[5] He also stated, "My hope is that this charter will be a kind of Ten Commandments, a Sermon on the Mount, that provides a guide for human behavior toward the environment, in the next century and beyond."[6]

As you read the opening paragraphs that form the preamble to the Earth Charter, it brings to mind the ancient pagan worship of Mother Earth, combined with the New Age movement. Here are a few of the "buzz" words: "interdependent world," "interconnected," "interrelated," "global interdependence," "worldcommunity," "global partnership," "global civilization," and "sustainable development." Read this radical document for yourself at *www.earthcharter.org*.

The sixteen general principles, which consist of another forty-seven subprinciples, in the Earth Charter give the details of how to use the "environmental crisis" for world government. Another statement made by Gorbachev sums it all up in a neat package: "The environmental crisis is the cornerstone for the New World Order."

Since the Antichrist will be in charge of the world government, he will need a world constitution. Guess what! There is already a world constitution drafted. In 1987 the World Constitution and Parliament Association (WCPA), located in Lakewood, Colorado, drafted this fifty-page document entitled "A Constitution for the Federation of Earth."[7]

The World Constitution and Parliament Association was founded back in 1959, and presently has over fifteen million members from more than eighty countries. The membership consists of prime ministers, ambassadors, key members of the United Nations, dignitaries, influential financiers and attorneys, as well as leading educators and religious leaders. WCPA also boasts a network of more than four hundred thirty organizations worldwide.[8] In reality, the WCPA is a storefront for one-worlders, United Nations, New Age organizations, and even the World Council of Churches.

Let's examine the World Constitution. One of its first statements is: "Responsible world government is at least forty-seven years overdue." There is also a "Partial List of World Problems," which the WCPA cites for needing a world government. Most of the "problems" deal with the environment, military disarmament, world hunger, and the economy. The World Constitution contains a preamble and nineteen articles. The preamble reads like a page out of a New Age occult manual. Here is a portion of it:

> Realizing that Humanity today has come to a turning point in history and that we are on the threshold of a new world order which promises to usher in an era of peace, prosperity, justice, and harmony. Conscious that humanity is one . . . and that the principles of unity in diversity is the basis for a new age. . . . Conscious of the inescapable reality that the greatest hope for the survival of life on earth is the establishment of a democratic world government we, citizens of the world, hereby resolve to establish a world federation to be governed in accordance with this constitution for the federation of Earth.

Articles I through III of the World Constitution cover the broad functions, basic structure, and organs of the world government. They will regulate virtually every aspect of life, from communications and transportation to world trade and all other global processes.

Article IV will prohibit and eliminate the design, testing, manufacture, sale, purchase, use, and possession of weapons of mass destruction. It will either prohibit or regulate all lethal weapons. This means there could be complete gun control and no more national defense. This article will also create a world financial banking and credit union, along with a World Economic Development Organization.

Amazingly, the first four articles of the World Constitution set up three out of the four world systems spoken of in Revelation 13, a world government (v. 7), a world military (v. 4), and a world economy (v. 16–18) which will be run by the world dictator or Antichrist.

Articles V and VI set up a world parliament and world executive. One of their functions would be to approve, amend, or reject international laws developed prior to the advent of world government. With a swipe of a pen, this article would do away with our God-given rights and our God-ordained U.S. Constitution and Bill of Rights.

Article VIII is the Integrative Complex. One of the seven agencies created under this branch is the World Boundaries and Election Administration. It will be headed by a ten-member commission, in addition to the senior administrator from ten World Magna Regions. This sounds like the end-time scenario of the ten kings and Antichrist in Daniel 7:24: "And the ten horns out of this kingdom are ten kings that shall arise: and another shall rise after them. . . ." Verse twenty-five goes on to tell us that the one individual (Antichrist) who rules over the other ten kings and the whole earth will blaspheme God, persecute the saints, change laws, and will rule the world for "a time and times and the dividing of time," which is three and one-half years according to the original Aramaic words in verse twenty-five.

That is the bad news, but here is the good news. Daniel 7:26–27 tells us that in the end, God will judge and destroy the Antichrist's kingdom and set up an everlasting kingdom:

> But the judgment shall sit, and they shall take away his dominion, to consume and to destroy it unto the end. And the kingdom and dominion, and the greatness of the kingdom under the whole heaven, shall be given to the people of the saints of the most High, whose kingdom is an everlasting kingdom, and all dominions shall serve and obey him.

If only the fifteen million members of the World Constitution and Parliament Association would read, heed, and accept the Word of God as truth, they could be a part of this everlasting kingdom. We need to pray for them.

Article IX sets up the World Judiciary, with a World Supreme Court and world judges, elected from the ten World Magna Regions.

Article X creates the Enforcement System that includes the World Police. That's right! The World Police. Does that send chills down your spine? According to sections A and B, the Enforcement System functions will be investigation, apprehension, arrest, prosecution, remedies, correction, and conflict resolution. Section C describes the World Police who will be responsible for searches, apprehension, and arrest of individuals responsible for violations of world law. Section D describes the "Means of Enforcement," which includes denial of financial credit, revocation of licenses, impounding of equipment, imprisonment, or isolation and other means, appropriate to the specific situation. I wonder what the "other means" could be?

This article reminds us of Revelation 13:17 where you will not be able to buy or sell, unless you have taken the mark of the beast (666).

Article XV, Section B, sets up a Primary World Capitol. We know from Revelation 17 and 18 this world capitol or city will be destroyed in one hour. Article XVII covers the ratification and implementation process of the World Constitution for the Federation of Earth. Section D issues an invitation to a very powerful worldwide organization to transfer personnel, facilities, equipment, resources, and allegiance to the Federation of Earth and to the world government thereof. Can you guess who it is? The United Nations! Section E states that all viable agencies of the United Nations including their personnel, facilities, and resources, shall be transferred to the World Government and reconstituted. This section is a radical change from the previous Section D, which only invited the United Nations to transfer everything over to the World Government. Sounds like a prearranged deal to me! The World Constitution ends with a picture of the United Nations logo, which sums up their true agenda: "to control the whole world."

The contents of this document, A Constitution for the Federation of Earth, are blatant enough that no further explanation is required, other than it goes hand in glove with the end-time scenario of Revelation 13. Will this world constitution be the one Antichrist will use? Only God knows! For more information on the world constitution, access their website at *www.wcpogren.org.*

There is one obstacle that is presently holding back the implementation of the world constitution and New World Order. It is our God-ordained U.S. Constitution and Bill of Rights. In the very near future, these precious documents which have given Americans freedoms, liberties, and rights for over two centuries could be removed completely, suspended indefinitely, or bypassed with a stroke of a pen. There are three ways this could be accomplished.

The first way is through executive orders issued by the president, which appear in the *Federal Register* for thirty days. If there is no challenge by Congress, the order becomes law. Sadly, most American citizens do not know that our republican form of government and the U.S. Constitution grants the president no lawmaking authority. Recall Article 1, Section 8, states: "All legislative [lawmaking] powers herein granted shall be vested in a Congress. . . ."

When a president creates a new law by executive order, our representative government is completely averted and any concept of checks and balances or separation of powers is no longer involved in the legislative process. Once again the bottom line is this: executive orders give the president the power to act as an unaccountable dictator.

The following are just a few of the shocking and frightening dictatorial powers that former President Bill Clinton has created.

Executive order 12919,[9] gives the president complete power during a declared "State of National Emergency" (real or manufactured) over all food resources, food resource facilities, farms and farm equipment, fertilizer, all sources of energy, including gas and electricity, all transportation, including your personal car, highways, trucks, buses, trains, airports, jets, seaports, all health resources, including hospitals, health supplies, and equipment, all metals and minerals, and all water resources. This is only one of three hundred executive orders President Clinton has issued. Most of them are nothing more than "power grabs" to bypass Congress and go directly to the Federal Emergency Management Agency (FEMA), or hand our national sovereignty to the United Nations, or give special rights to homosexuals and the environmentalists. One of Clinton's advisors, Paul Begala, smugly remarked: "Stroke of the pen. Law of the land. Kinda cool." Future presidents will also have these same dictatorial powers at their fingertips.

The second way our U.S. Constitution could be done away with is a constitutional convention. Let me set the stage by explaining what happened at the first and only constitutional convention. At this convention, held in Philadelphia, Pennsylvania, in 1789, our Founding Fathers threw out the existing government, which was the Articles of Confederation, and then wrote a totally new constitution.[10] This first convention also set up what is called a legal precedent. In other words, if another constitutional convention is called, the same thing could happen today. With the stroke of a pen, our government leaders could throw out our existing government and draft a new one.

A new constitution called the "Newstates of America Constitution" has already been drafted by over one hundred liberal and prominent professors and attorneys.[11] A tax-exempt foundation with the misleading name Center for the Study of Democratic Institutions began writing this "abortive" constitution in 1964. This subversive constitution pretends to follow the language of our U.S. Constitution. It contains a preamble and twelve articles.[12] According to the preamble, we are no longer called the United States of America, but the "Newstates of America." This goes right along with the New World Order! In a nutshell, this Soviet-style constitution takes away our God-given unalienable rights. It gives us government privileges under a police state. Here are a few examples:

Article I, Section 8 states: "The practice of religion shall be privileged." Did you catch that? Privileged? A privilege is like your drivers license; it can be taken away. Section 8 also states, "But no religion shall be imposed by some upon others." Pastors, listen closely! Each time you preach, you impose your religion on others. Unless your preaching is politically correct and not considered a hate crime, will it be tolerated under the Newstates Constitution?

Also, in Section 8 under "Responsibilities" we find: "There shall be a responsibility to avoid violence and to keep the peace; for this reason the bearing of arms or the possession of lethal weapons shall be confined to the police, members of the armed forces, and those licensed under law." This is complete federal gun control.

Section 11 states: "Education shall be provided at public expense only for those who meet appropriate tests of eligibility." I wonder what kind of "appropriate tests" there will be. Who will prepare them? You can be sure the revisionists will include situation ethics, values clarification, alternative lifestyles, and political correctness. Notice, there is nothing mentioned about private Christian schools or home schooling. I wonder why? Because there will not be any Christian education unless it is state-approved.

Article VIII, Section 14C states: "The Supreme Court may decide whether international law as recognized in treaties, United Nations agreements, or arrangements with other nations, has been ignored or violated." Once again America would be put at the mercy of the United Nations.

The other ten articles, when read closely, will set America up for a police state under a dictatorship in the New World Order.

Maybe some of you are thinking our government officials would never allow the Newstates Constitution to replace our God-ordained U.S. Constitution. How many times have many of our leaders stated: "We need to reinvent government"? On March 4, 1993, former President Bill Clinton stated:

"We intend to redesign, to reinvent, to reinvigorate the entire national government."[13] Former Vice-President Al Gore stated: "What was written with quill pen is outdated, and we need to reinvent government."

Let me tell you how close we are to calling for a constitutional convention! According to Article V of our U.S. Constitution, two-thirds, or thirty-four, of the states must call for a constitutional convention. Presently there are twenty-nine active calls on the books.[14] If five more states call for a constitutional convention, our existing U.S. Constitution could be thrown out. A new constitution could be drafted and approved.

The third way to do away with or suspend our U.S. Constitution is by martial law, when there is a declared State of National Emergency. Martial law is simply the rule of the military when the civil government can no longer maintain law and order. Under martial law, the Constitution is suspended and legal protections we enjoy such as *habeas corpus* (right to trial by jury) can be suspended and people can be arrested and imprisoned indefinitely without charges. All First Amendment rights are suspended, and censorship of the press, TV, radio, and the Internet can be imposed. House-to-house searches and seizures of firearms could also be conducted.

A crisis, real or staged, can justify a State of National Emergency and martial law. For example, a financial collapse, nationwide bank run, terrorist attack, or a computer shutdown that causes the power grid, transportation, or banks to fail. In the 1992 Los Angeles riots, the people begged for martial law to stop the pain. In 1933 Americans yielded their freedoms to Franklin Roosevelt during the Great Depression when he declared a State of National Emergency. In that same year, the German people willingly surrendered their freedom to Adolph Hitler in a State of National Emergency after Hitler and his Brown Shirts burned the German parliament and blamed it on the communists.[15]

The bottom line is: The legal authority for martial law and the suspension of our U.S. Constitution is in place through executive orders.

On September 11, 2001 all of us watched on TV the horrible and shocking terrorist attack on New York's twin World Trade Centers and the Pentagon. Even though a national "State of Emergency" was not called, we can see how quickly things can happen for ushering us into a global New World Order.

Interestingly, the first two jets hit the World Trade Centers which were symbols of the world's economy. The third jet was crashed into the Pentagon, a symbol of the world's greatest military. A fourth jet crashed into the earth in western Pennsylvania that was headed for the White House or capitol, a symbol of the world's greatest government.

Finally, a national day of prayer was called in Washington, D.C., with Jews, Moslems, and Christians speakers, furthering a world religion coming together.

All four of these world systems including the government, military, economy, and religion were represented in the "Terrorist's Attacks on America." Interestingly, the newest phrase being used for the New World Order is the "global coalition."

Sooner or later, another world crisis will come on the scene to justify the New World Order and a global government, military, economy, and religion with a world dictator in charge. Just read Revelation 13.

In case it is hard for you to believe what you have just read, wait until I give you the following eye-opening and sobering information. Some time ago there was legislation passed that could possibly be the foundation for decapitation. On March 26, 1991, H. J. Resolution 104 was signed into law. The joint resolution of the House and Senate established Public Law No. 102-14 and designated March 26, 1991, as "Education Day, U.S.A."

This law was allegedly to honor Rabbi Menachem Scheerson, a great spiritual leader, on his ninetieth birthday. Written into all the "whereas's" were incorporated two references calling for the return to the ethical values of the "Seven Noahide Laws." As we make a cursory examination of the laws, we do not see anything blatantly objectionable. Neither will you find any call for decapitation in this harmless appearing document, but beware, there is much more than meets the eye.

When you dig into the historical documents of the ancient Jewish Talmud with reference to the Noahide laws, guess what you will find· "decapitation" for breaking certain commandments.

Before we go any further, our government did not call for the establishment of capital punishment by decapitation in Public Law No. 102-14, but I believe the foundation for such a law has been laid.

The Noahide Laws are defined in the *Jewish Encyclopedia* (KTAV Publishing House, Inc.), pages 648–49, followed by the prescribed punishment:

> LAWS, NOACHIAN, (Hate Crimes) 2 Thessalonians 2:4: (1) not to worship
> idols; (2) not to blaspheme the name of God; (3) to establish courts of jus-
> tice; (4) not to kill; (5) not to commit adultery; and (6) not to rob. . . . The
> prevalent opinion in the Talmud is that there are only seven laws which are
> binding upon all mankind. . . . In the elaboration of these seven Noachian
> laws, and in assigning punishments for their transgression, the Rabbis are
> sometime more lenient and sometimes more rigorous with Noachidae [non-
> Jews] than with Israelites. With but a few exceptions, the punishment meted
> out to a Noachid for the transgression of any of the seven laws is decapita-
> tion, the least painful of the four modes of execution of criminals. The many
> formalities of procedures essential when the accused is an Israelite need
> not be observed in the case of the Noachid. The latter may be convicted on
> the testimony of one witness, even on that of relatives, but not on that of a
> woman. He need have had no warning from the witnesses; and a single
> judge may pass sentence on him. . . .

Under the Noahide laws during the Tribulation period, Christians could be
considered guilty of violating the blasphemy law. Christians believe that Jesus,
the Christ, is God in the flesh (John 1:1, 14). Recall that Antichrist will "sit
in the temple of God, shewing himself that he is God" (2 Thessalonians 2:4).
If a Christian would not worship the Antichrist, they could be found guilty
of blasphemy.

In the July-August issue of *The Gap* newsletter, published by the Noahide
movement, the lead article revealed that there is pressure being applied for
worldwide recognition of the seven Noahide Laws. Professor of International
Law Ernest Easterly, Southern University Law Center, said: "With further
recognition by other nations and international courts, the Seven Noahide
Laws should become the cornerstone of a truly civilized international legal
order."

Welcome to the New World Order! Presently we are seeing the institution of so-called "hates crimes" around the world. This hate crime legislation could be the precursor to the Noahide laws for beheading. I want to give
you some information about how this legislation is already being used against
Christians.

In 1988 a Swedish pastor preached about Sodom and Gomorrah with biblical references from Genesis 19. This pastor also preached that homosexuality was a sin. There was a homosexual present in the church service that day. Several months later this pastor served a jail sentence because he had violated Sweden's "anti-hate statute" that protects groups such as homosexuals from "verbal violence."

"Hate crimes," "verbal violence," and "hurtful speech" against groups of people are already on the books in West Germany, Britain, Israel, and Canada. In Canada there is a five thousand dollar fine and a two-year prison sentence for a person found guilty of "defaming" an "identifiable group."[16]

Amazingly, Communists, abortionists, and radical feminists are not seen as hate groups, but Christians are.

In 1990 our U.S. Congress passed the "Hate Crimes Statistic Act" that requires states to determine if crimes committed in their jurisdiction are motivated by prejudice. This information goes into a national data bank. The Anti-Defamation League is one of the movers and shakers of hate crime legislation. They have thirty nationwide branches around the world with the national hub in New York City.

A new bill, S.622 entitled "Hate Crimes Prevention Act" was introduced in 2001. This act gives federal jurisdiction for violent hate crimes.[17] It can only be a short time until America puts Christians in jail for so-called "hate crimes against an identifiable group." Jesus said in Matthew 24:9, "Then shall they deliver you up to be afflicted, and shall kill you, and ye shall be hated of all nations for my name's sake," and in Luke 21:12 ". . . They shall lay their hands on you, and persecute you, delivering you to the synagogues, and into prisons, being brought before kings and rulers for my name's sake."

For much more detailed information on the New World Order, may I please recommend to you my video and book entitled *World Dominion: From the Tower of Babel to the Mark of the Beast.* This hard-hitting video and book will tell you how the coming world dictator will identify, track, and locate billions of people. See the world's first human cyborg, belly-button microchips for newborn babies, the "Digital Angel" implant, and the most frightening microchip, the "Soul Catcher 2025."

Learn about the United Nations and their "land grabs" through what is called "U.N. Biosphere Reserves" and "U.N. World Heritage Sites." Discover the plan for uniting the world's religions through the sinister "Global Ethic" and deceptive "World Scripture" bible. To become informed on these issues and many others, get a copy of the video and book *World Dominion* today.

In closing let me relate from Holy Scripture what has happened to America. First, we as Christians have not passed on our godly heritage to the next generation as commanded in Psalm 78:1–8. The results of not passing on our godly heritage to the next generation is found in Judges 2:10: ". . . And there arose another generation after them, which knew not the Lord, nor yet the works which he had done for Israel."

A large generation from the 1960s arose in America that "knew not the Lord." That generation took off their sandals, cut their hair, went to secular atheistic universities, put on a suit and tie, and are now running the nation.

Presently, according to Hosea 4:6 ". . . My people are destroyed for lack of knowledge. . . ." We know how to put a man on the moon, clone animals and maybe humans, but how many Americans really know God and Jesus Christ personally and intimately? The next step down the slippery slope is found in Judges 21:25: ". . . Every man did that which was right in his own eyes." Just read the newspapers or listen to the latest rulings handed down by courts. There are no absolutes! America has forgotten God!

The straw that will break the camel's (or America's in this case) back is found in Psalm 9:17: "The wicked shall be turned into hell, and all nations that forget God." God is not a respecter of persons (Romans 2:11) or nations.

Apart from an old-fashion Holy Ghost revival and godly repentance, America is on the edge of being turned into hell. God can accomplish this in different ways. He can turn us over to the heathens or foreigners as He did the children of Israel. He can send an economic collapse or any of a number of other national calamities.

What can we as Christians do? The same question is asked in Psalm 11:3: "If the foundations be destroyed, what can the righteous do?"

First we need to follow the wisdom of 1 Chronicles 12:32, "And the children of Issachar which were men that had understanding of the times, to know what Israel ought to do." After meditating on the Holy Scriptures that have been used in this book, along with the rest of the information, you personally have an "understanding of the times" concerning our nation. You are no longer "destroyed for a lack of knowledge."

Second we need to get involved in our sphere of influence. Remember we are to be the "salt and light" in a "crooked and perverse nation" (Matthew 5:13–14; Philippians 2:15). We are also to "occupy till Jesus comes" (Luke 19:13). You could start by giving this book to your family, friends, neighbors, pastor, relatives, public officials, or placing a copy in your local church, Christian bookstore, or library. Vote for godly men and women who have proven track records. Write and call you congressmen concerning laws that infringe on our God-given rights and freedoms. Write letters to the editor of your newspaper. Call in and speak out on radio talk programs. Consider running for a local position in your city, such as a school board member or city councilman. Ask the Lord in prayer specifically what He would have you do in the area of biblical government.

Third, the most effective political action you could take would be to lead your neighbor(s) to Christ. Do you lead people to Jesus Christ? Jesus said in Mark 16:15, ". . . Go ye into all the world, and preach the gospel to every creature." We need to win people to Christ. Proverbs 11:30 states ". . . He that winneth souls is wise."

Fourth, we need to pray for a heaven-sent revival according to the principles in 2 Chronicles 7:14, "If my people, which are called by my name, shall humble themselves, and pray, and seek my face, and turn from their wicked ways; then will I hear from heaven, and will forgive their sin, and will heal their land."

This verse is speaking to God's people. We will not have revival in the White House or the schoolhouse till we first have revival in the church house. Revival starts with you and me. Maybe you need to get on your knees before God right now and get totally right. First Peter 4:17 states "For the time is come that judgment must begin at the house of God. . . ."

Maybe you are not sure if you are a Christian, or maybe you know that you are not a Christian. If Jesus were to come back today, do you know for sure He would take you back to heaven? What if you died today? Where would you spend eternity? In heaven or hell?

The only way to have your sins forgiven and have everlasting life with the assurance of heaven, is by receiving God's gift of eternal life. That's correct. Eternal life is a free gift to everyone (Romans 6:23). God wants to give you that free gift of eternal life right now, but you must first admit to God you have sinned against Him (Romans 3:23). The penalty for sin is separation from God forever in the lake of fire, which is the second death (Revelation 20:14–15).

God is not willing that any should perish, and to prove it He sent His only begotten Son, Jesus Christ, who died on the cross for your sin and mine (John 3:16). Please, I beg you right now, get on your knees and tell God in your own words that you have sinned against Him. You do believe Jesus died, was buried, and rose again (Romans 10:9). Tell Him you want the gift of eternal life, Jesus Christ. "Whosoever [that means you] shall call upon the name of the Lord shall be saved" (Romans 10:13). Please ask Jesus Christ to come into your heart and life right now. I trust you will settle your eternal destiny because, ". . . now is the accepted time; behold, now is the day of salvation" (2 Corinthians 6:2). I will be praying for you.

Thank you, and God bless!

For more information, questions, a product and price list, or just to let me know that you have received Jesus Christ as your Savior, write to:

Vaughn Shatzer
P.O. Box 1113
Hagerstown, MD 21741

Endnotes

Chapter 1: Government is Ordained of God (Romans 13:1)

1. Noah Webster, *History of the United States*, p. 1. S. Babcock, New Haven, 1836.
2. David Barton, *Keys to Good Government*, pp. 6–7.
3. Ibid., p 6.
4. Ibid., p 6.
5. Jedediah Morse's election sermon given at Charleston, MA on April 25, 1799. Taken from *Education and the Founding Fathers*, p. 15. David Barton, Wall Builders, Aledo, TX, 1993.
6. Steven Morris, *Los Angeles Times*, August 3, 1995, p. B-9.
7. Steven Morris, professor of physics at Los Angeles Harbor College, article entitled "Free Inquiry," p. 12.
8. *Journals of the Continental Congress 1774–1789*. Government Printing Office, Washington, D.C., 1905.
9. Charles Francis Adams, ed., *Letters of John Adams Addressed to His Wife*, Vol. 1, pp. 23–24. Charles C. Little and James Brown, Boston, 1841.
10. First Prayer in Congress, Library of Congress, Washington, D.C.
11. *Journals of the Continental Congress, 1774–1789*, Vol. XXIII, p. 574.
12. Cover page for the *Bible of the Revolution*, either 1782 original or the 1968 reprint by Arno Press, New York.
13. *Public School of Washington*, Vol. 1, p. 5. Columbia Historical Society, Washington, D.C., 1897.
14. David Barton, *Spiritual Heritage*, p. 25. Wall Builders, Aledo, TX, 2000.
15. The name of the Bible Society of Philadelphia has been changed to Pennsylvania Bible Society, 701 Walnut St., Philadelphia, PA 19106. Phone 215-922-6779.
16. *The Tract Primer*, American Tract Society, 150 Nassau St., New York, NY.
77. *Publications of the American Tract Society*, Vol. 1. 1813.

Chapter 2: The Bible and Early Martyrs (A.D. 1200–A.D. 1600)

1. Mark A. Beliles and Stephen K. McDowell, *America's Providential History*, p. 42. 1989, Providence Foundation, Charlottesville, VA.
2. David Barton, *Spiritual Heritage*, p. 14.
3. *America's Providential History*, p. 42.
4. Harold J. Chadwick, John Foxe, *The New Foxe's Book of Martyrs*. Bride-Logos Publishers, Gainsville, FL.
5. R. W. Thompson, *The Papacy and the Civil Power*, p. 82. New York, 1876.
6. *America's Providential History*, p. 42.
7. James Kennedy, *The Pilgrims Speak Today*, p. 5, Coral Ridge Ministries, Fort Lauderdale, FL.
8. *America's Providential History*, pp. 43–44.

9. Ibid., pp. 43–44.
10. Ibid., pp. 44–45.
11. Ibid., p. 53.
12. Ibid., p. 54.
13. Ibid., p. 48.
14. David Barton, *Spiritual Heritage,* pp. 13–14.
15. James Kennedy, *The Pilgrims Speak Today,* p. 5.
16. *America's Providential History,* p. 56.
17. Benjamin Harris, *New England Primer.* Boston, 1777.
18. *America's Providential History,* p. 56.
19. Reverend Samuel Rutherford, *Lex Rex,* 1644.
20. William Federer, *America's God and Country Encyclopedia of Quotations,* p. 546. Fame Publishing, Coppell, TX, 1994.

Chapter 3: America Was Founded as a Christian Nation

1. William Blackstone, *Commentaries on the Laws of England,* Vol. 1, pp. 41–42. 1856.
2. Ibid., Vol. IV, p. 42.
3. Ibid., p. 41.
4. Ibid., Vol. I, p. 41 [3].
5. Ibid., Vol. IV, p. 194.
6. Ibid., p. 210.
7. Ibid., Vol. I, p. 441.
8. Ibid., Vol. IV, p. 219.
9. Ibid., pp. 41–65.
10. Ibid., pp. 44–50.
11. Noah Webster, *History of the United States,* pp. 309–310.
12. A. J. Dallas, *Reports of Cases and Adjudged in the Courts of Pennsylvania,* p. 39, *Respublica v. John Roberts,* Pennsylvania Supreme Court, 1778. Printed for P. Byrne, Pennsylvania, 1806.
13. *Respublica v. John Roberts,* Vol. 2, pp. 34–37.
14. *Jane Doe v. Santa Fe Independent School District,* C.A. No. G-95-176, Galveston, TX, 1995.
15. *State of Florida v. George Broxon,* Walton County Florida, Case No. 90-0293-CF, pp. 3–4, 1992.
16. *Runkel v. Winemiller,* 4H and McH. 276, Maryland Supreme Court, 1799.
17. *Church of the Holy Trinity. v. United States,* 143 U.S. pp. 457, 470–471, 1892.
18. *Torcaso v. Watkins,* 367 U.S. 488, 1961.
19. *United States v. Seeger,* 380 U.S. 163, 1965.
20. *Malnak v. Yogi,* 440 F. Supp. 1284, D.C., NY, 1977.
21. *Theriault v. Silber,* 547 F. 2d 1279, 5th Cir., 1977.
22. *County of Allegheny v. ACLU,* 106 L. Ed. 2d 472, 1989.
23. *Grove v. Mead School District,* 753 F. 2d, 1528, 9th Cir., 1985, cert. denied, 474 U.S. 826.
24. Bob Larson, *New Book of Cults,* p. 464. Tyndale House Publishers, Wheaton, IL, 1989.
25. *Torcaso v. Watkins,* p. 11.
26. *Random House Dictionary of the English Language,* unabridged 2nd edition.

Random House, New York, 1987.

27. *People v. Ruggles*, 8 Johns 545, New York Supreme Ct., 1811.

28. Ibid., p. 219.

29. Ibid., p. 219.

30. *Grove v. Mead School District.*

31. *Commonwealth v. Sharpless and Others*, 2 Serg and R 91, Pennsylvania Supreme Court, pp. 90, 92–93, 101. 1815.

32. *Miller v. California*, 413 U.S. pp. 15, 27. 1973.

33. James Lambert, *Porn in America*, p. 16. Huntington House Publishers, Lafayette, LA.

34. Ibid., p. 21

35. Ibid., p. 137; *Time* magazine, March 30, 1992, p. 53.

36. Ibid., p. 75; *Time* magazine, September 19, 1988, p. 44.

37. *U.S. News and World Report*, February 10, 1997.

38. Ibid.

39. Beverly LaHaye, "Flyer 2001." Concerned Women for America, 1015 15th St. NW, Suite 1100, Washington, D.C. 20005

40. Dr. Don Boys, Indiana Representative, *Liberalism: A Rope of Sand*, p. 65. Sword of the Lord Publishers, 1979.

41. *Pornography: A Report*, p. 19. American Family Association, P.O. Drawer 2440, Tupelo, MS 38803.

42. James Lambert, *Porn in America*, pp. 93. 94, 115, 119, 138.

43. *Vidal v. Girards Executors*, 43 U.S. pp. 126, 133, 143, 175, 200. 1844.

44. Silus Andrus, *Code of 1650, Being a Compilation of the Earliest Laws and Orders of the General Court of Connecticut.* Hartford, 1822.

45. *Abington v. Schempp*, 374 U.S. 203, 1963.

46. Ibid., p. 209.

47. *Engel v. Vitale*, 370 U.S. 421, 422, 1962.

48. *Stone v. Graham*, 449 U.S. 39, 1980.

49. *Bible In the News*, May 2001, p. 9. Southwest Radio Church Ministries, P.O. Box 100, Bethany, OK 73008. Phone 800-652 1144.

50. *Murphy v. Ramsey*, 114 U.S. 15, 1885.

51. Mike Wingfield, *Prophecy Today*, February 2001, p. 5. P.O. Box 210, Boones Mill, VA 24065.

52. Ibid., p. 6.

53. David Barton, *Wall Builder Report*, Spring 1996, p. 4.

54. *Washington Times*, August 21, 1997.

55. *The Weekly Standard*, August 19, 1996, p. 21.

56. *Education Newsline*, Winter 1998, p. 2. National Association of Christian Education Educators, Costa Mesa, CA.

57. James Kennedy, Newsletter, August 31, 1995, p. 3.

58. Ibid., Special Report, 1996.

59. Dr. John Willke, *Life Issues*, Vol. 1405, November 22, 1996. P.O. Box 31006, Cincinnati, OH 45231.

60. Tim Wildmon, American Family Association, "Boycott Disney flyer," 1996.

61. Ibid. "A.F.A. flyer," 1997; *U.S. News and World Report*, February 10, 1997.

62. *Public Opinion*, November 28, 1997, Chambersburg, PA.

63. Jerry Falwell, Newsletter, September 26, 1995 Lynchburg, VA.

64. *Blackstone's Commentaries on Law,* Vol. IV, pp. 215–216.
65. *The Writings of George Washington,* March 10, 1778, Bicentennial Edition, March 1 through May 31, 1778, Vol. 11, pp. 83–84. Published by the U.S. Government Printing Office, 1934. Also, John Trussel, Jr., *Epic on the Schuylkill, Commonwealth of Pennsylvania,* p. 23. Historical and Museum Commission, Harrisburg, PA, 1992.
66. John F. McManus, *Changing Commands,* pp. 61–68. The John Birch Society, Appleton, WI, 1995.
67. *Roe v. Wade,* 410 U.S. 113, 1973.
68. Dr. John Willke, *Love Them Both,* p. 33. 1997.
69. Dr. John Willke, *Abortion Questions & Answers,* Vol. VII. 1990.
70. *Blackstone's Commentaries on Law,* Vol. IV, p. 198 (31).
71. Dr. James Kennedy, Coral Ridge Ministries Newsletter, August 2001, p 1.
72. Ibid., February 2000, p. 1.
73. Ibid., June 2000.
74. Jay Sekulow, Office of the Chief Counsel American Medical News by Diane M. Gianelli, March 3, 1997.
75. Dr. James Kennedy, Coral Ridge Ministries Newsletter, February 2000, p 1.
76. Ibid., Newsletter, "Baby Body Parts for Sale," 1999.
77. Ibid., "Copy of Baby Body Parts List with prices," 1999.
78. Dr. John Willke, *Assisted Suicide & Euthanasia Past & Present,* p. 123. Hayes Publishing Co., Cincinnati, OH, 1999.
79. Ibid., p. 1.
80. Ibid., pp. 9, 11, 70–71.
81. Ibid., pp. 89, 90.
82. Ibid., p. 132.

Chapter 4: If the Foundations Be Destroyed (Psalm 11:3)
1. David Barton, *Original Intent,* p. 228.
2. Ibid.
3. *Cantwell v. State of Connecticut,* 310 U.S. 296, 1940.
4. David Barton, *Original Intent,* p. 198.
5. Brian Barkley, *Nation Adrift* video, 1996.
6. Ibid.
7. James Sedlak, *Cumulative Number of Surgical Abortions at Planned Parenthood,* chart by STOPP International, 2000.
8. Planned Parenthood, 1998–99 Annual Report, Hayes Publishing Co., 2001.
9. Dr. John Willke, *Why Can't We Love Them Both,* p 113. 1997.
10. *Lemon v. Kurtzman,* 403 U.S. 602, 1971.

Chapter 5: We Ought to Obey God Rather Than Men (Acts 5:29)
1. David Barton, *Original Intent,* p. 101.

Chapter 6: The "Black Regiment" of American Preachers
1. Mark A. Beliles and Steven K. McDowell, *America's Providential History,* p, 143, 1994.
2. David Barton, *Original Intent,* p. 86.
3. Peter Kershaw, *In Caesar's Grip,* p. 32. Heal Our Land Ministries, 2000.

4. Ibid., p. 32.
5. Ibid., p. 32.
6. *Citizens Rule Book*, p. 15. Whitten Printers, Pheonix, AZ.
7. *America's Providential History*, pp. 122, 137.
8. David Barton, *Original Intent*, pp. 104–105.
9. W. P. Breed, *Presbyterians and the Revolution*, p. 85.
10. H. Niles, *Principles and Acts*, p. 480.
11. J. Franklin Jameson, *The American Revolution Considered as a Social Movement*, pp. 91–92.

Chapter 7: Biblical Duties and Responsibilities of Rulers (Romans 13:3-4)

1. William Bradford, *History of Plimoth Plantation*, written in 1647. 1901 Edition.
2. *America's Providential History*, p 121.
3. Ibid., pp. 121, 122.
4. David Barton, *Original Intent*, pp. 119–120. Edward Kendall, *Travels in America*, Vol. 1, pp. 3–5, 1809.
5. *American Political Writing During the Founding Era 1760–1805*, Vol. 1 & 2, and *Political Sermons of the American Founding Era 1730–1805*, Vol. 1 & 2. Liberty Fund, 8335 Allison Pointe Trail, Suite 300, Indianapolis, Indiana, 46250, 1991.
6. Ibid., *Political Sermons*, Vol. 1, pp. 138–177.
7. Ibid., *Political Writing*, Vol. 1, pp. 410–448.
8. David Barton, *Original Intent*, pp. 103–104, election sermon, first day of election, March 12, 1778 at Windsor, Newburyport, John Mycall, 1778, p. 29.
9. Verna Hall, *The Christian History of Constitution of the U.S.A.*, p. 252. Foundation for American Christian Education, San Francisco, CA, 1985.
10. William Federer, *America's God and Country*, p. 177, 1994. Verna Hall, *Christian History of the Constitution*, F.A.C.E., p. 253. David Barton, *Original Intent*, p, 79.
11. William Federer, *America's God and Country*, p. 177.
12. Verna Hall, *Christian History of the Constitution*, F.A.C.E., pp. 252, 253.
13. Ibid., p. 252.
14. Ibid., p. 257.
15. James Kennedy, *Why Reclaiming America?*, p. 6, 2000.
16. *The Debates and Proceedings in Congress of the United States, Washington*, Gales and Seaton, 1851, Sixth Congress, Second Session, p. 797, December 4, 1800.
17. Ellis Sandoz, *Political Sermons of the American Founding Era*, pp. 1572–1596. 1990.
18. William Jay, *The Life of John Jay*, Vol. II, p. 376. J & J Harper, New York, 1833 letter to John Murray Jr. on October 12, 1816.
19. David Barton, *Keys to Good Government* video and audio cassette tapes, 1990.
20. Noah Webster, *Letters to a Young Gentleman Commencing His Education*, pp. 18–19, Letter 1. New Haven, S. Convers, 1823.
21. Library of Congress, Washington, D.C., David Barton, *Original Intent*, pp. 39, 321–322.
22. Library of Congress, Washington D.C.

Chapter 8: Biblical Functions of Government (Romans 13:3 & 1 Peter 2:14)

1. Steven H. Gifis, *Burron's Law Dictionary*, 1996.

Chapter 9: The New World Order

1. Vaughn Shatzer, *World Dominion,* pp. 95–135. Hearthstone Publishing, Oklahoma City, 2000.
2. Terry Cook, *The Mark of the New World Order,* p. 9. Virtue International Publishing, Indianapolis, IN.
3. Rob Lindsted, Ph.D., *Can You Really Know Your Future?,* p 53. Bible Truth, Wichita, Kansas.
4. Professional audio tapes recorded live at State of the World Forum by Sound True Recordings, Boulder, Colorado.
5. Mikhail Gorbachev, "The Earth Charter" speech, Rio+5 Forum, March 18, 1997.
6. Ibid. "Environment: Act Globally, Not Nationally," interview with the *Los Angeles Times.*
7. World Constitution and Parliament Association, 8800 West 14th St., Lakewood, Colorado 80215.
8. Gary Kah, *The New World Religion,* pp. 84–85, 167. Hope International Publishing, Noblesville, Indiana.
9. Vaughn Shatzer, *World Dominion,* pp. 145–163, or on the internet at *www.whitehouse.com.*
10. David Barton, *Original Intent,* p 110.
11. Liberty Library, 300 Independence Ave. S.E., Washington D.C. 2003, Rexford G. Tugwell, Harper and Row, 1974.
12. Newstates of American Constitution, Liberty Library, p 1.
13. Joan Veon, *The United Nations' Global Straitjacket,* p 85. Hearthstone Publishing, Oklahoma City, OK.
14. Joan Collins, *Constitution in Crisis,* pp. 36–37. Hearthstone Publishing, Oklahoma City, OK.
15. Don McAlvany, *Storm Warning,* p. 195.
16. Theodore Winston Pike, from his video, *Hate Laws-Making Criminals of Christians,* National Prayer Network, P.O. Box 828, Clackamas, OR 97015, *www.Truthtellers.org.*
17. Ibid.

Part II

The Documents

Document A

Church of the Holy Trinity v. U.S.

143 U.S. 457, 12 S.Ct. 511, 36 L.Ed. 226

Feb. 29, 1892

In error to the circuit court of the United States for
the southern district of New York. Reversed.

No. 143. Argued and submitted January 7, 1892.

Decided February 29, 1892

The act of February 26, 1885, "to prohibit the importation and migration of
foreigners and aliens under contract or agreement to perform labor in the
United States, its Territories, and the District of Columbia," 23 Stat. 332, c.
164, does not apply to a contract between an alien, residing out of the United
States, and a religious society incorporated under the laws of a State, whereby
he engages to remove to the United States and to enter into the service of
the society as its rector of minister.

The case is stated in the opinion.

Mr. Seaman Miller, for plaintiff in error.
Mr. Assistant Attorney General Maury, for the United States.

Mr. Justice Brewer delivered the opinion of the court.

Plaintiff in error is a corporation duly organized and incorporated as a religious society under the laws of the state of New York. E. Walpole Warren
was, prior to September, 1887, an alien residing in England. In that month
the plaintiff in error made a contract with him, by which he was to remove

to the city of New York, and enter into its service as rector and pastor; and, in pursuance of such contract, Warren did so remove and enter upon such service. It is claimed by the United States that this contract on the part of the plaintiff in error was forbidden by chapter 164, 23 St. p. 332; and an action was commenced to recover the penalty prescribed by that act. The circuit court held that the contract was within the prohibition of the statute, and rendered judgment accordingly, (36 Fed. Rep. 303,) and the single question presented for our determination is whether it erred in that conclusion.

The first section describes the act forbidden, and is in these words:

"Be it enacted by the senate and house of representatives of the United States of America, in congress assembled, that from and after the passage of this act it shall be unlawful for any person, company, partnership, or corporation, in any manner whatsoever, to prepay the transportation, or in any way assist or encourage the importation or migration, of any alien or aliens, any foreigner or foreigners, into the United States, its territories, or the District of Columbia, under contract or agreement, parol or special, express or implied, made previous to the importation or migration of such alien or aliens, foreigner or foreigners, to perform labor or service of any kind in the United States, its territories, or the District of Columbia."

It must be conceded that the act of the corporation is within the letter of this section, for the relation of rector to his church is one of service, and implies labor on the one side with compensation on the other. Not only are the general words "labor" and "service" both used, but also, as it were to guard against any narrow interpretation and emphasize a breadth of meaning, to them is added "of any kind;" and, further, as noticed by the circuit judge in his opinion, the fifth section, which makes specific exceptions, among them professional actors, artists, lecturers, singers, and domestic servants, strengthens the idea that every other kind of labor and service was intended to be reached by the first section. While there is great force to this reasoning, we cannot think congress intended to denounce with penalties a transaction like that in the present case. It is a familiar rule that a thing may be within the letter of the statute and yet not within the statute, because not within its spirit nor within the intention of its makers. This has been often asserted, and the Reports are full of cases illustrating its application. This is not the substitution of the will of the judge for that of the legislator; for

frequently words of general meaning are used in a statute, words broad
enough to include an act in question, and yet a consideration of the whole
legislation, or of the circumstances surrounding its enactment, or of the
absurd results which follow from giving such broad meaning to the words,
makes it unreasonable to believe that the legislator intended to include the
particular act. As said in *Stradling* v. *Morgan*, Plow. 205: "From which cases
it appears that the sages of the law heretofore have construed statutes quite
contrary to the letter in some appearance, and those statutes which comprehend all things in the letter they have expounded to extend to but some
things, and those which generally prohibit all people from doing such an act
they have interpreted to permit some people to do it, and those which include every person in the letter they have adjudged to reach to some persons
only, which expositions have always been founded upon the intent of the
legislature, which they have collected sometimes by considering the cause
and necessity of making the act, sometimes by comparing one part of the act
with another, and sometimes by foreign circumstances."

In *Pier Co.* v. *Hannam,* 3 Barn. & Ald. 266, Abbott, C. J., quotes from
Lord Coke as follows: "Acts of parliament are to be so construed as no man
that is innocent or free from injury or wrong be, by a literal construction,
punished or endangered." In the case of *State* v. *Clark,* 29 N. J. Law, 96, 99,
it appeared that an act had been passed, making it a misdemeanor to willfully break down a fence in the possession of another person. Clark was
indicted under that statute. The defense was that the act of breaking down
the fence, though willful, was in the exercise of a legal right to go upon his
own lands. The trial court rejected the testimony offered to sustain the defense, and the supreme court held that this ruling was error. In its opinion
the court used this language: "The act of 1855, in terms, makes the willful
opening, breaking down, or injuring of any fences belonging to or in the
possession of any other person a misdemeanor. In what sense is the term
'willful' used? In common parlance, 'willful' is used in the sense of 'intentional,' as distinguished from 'accidental' or 'involuntary.' Whatever one does
intentionally, he does willfully. Is it used in that sense in this act? Did the
legislature intend to make the intentional opening of a fence for the purpose
of going upon the land of another indictable, if done by permission or for a
lawful purpose? . . . We cannot suppose such to have been the actual intent.

To adopt such a construction would put a stop to the ordinary business of life. The language of the act, if construed literally, evidently leads to an absurd result. If a literal construction of the words of a statute be absurd, the act must be so construed as to avoid the absurdity. The court must restrain the words. The object designed to be reached by the act must limit and control the literal import of the terms and phrases employed." In *U.S.* v. *Kirby,* 7 Wall. 482, 486, the defendants were indicted for the violation of an act of congress providing "that if any person shall knowingly and willfully obstruct or retard the passage of the mail, or of any driver or carrier, or of any horse or carriage carrying the same, he shall, upon conviction, for every such offense, pay a fine not exceeding one hundred dollars." The specific charge was that the defendants knowingly and willfully retarded the passage of one Farris, a carrier of the mail, while engaged in the performance of his duty, and also in like manner retarded the steamboat *Gen. Buell,* at that time engaged in carrying the mail. To this indictment the defendants pleaded specially that Farris had been indicted for murder by a court of competent authority in Kentucky; that a bench-warrant had been issued and placed in the hands of the defendant Kirby, the sheriff of the county, commanding him to arrest Farris, and bring him before the court to answer to the indictment; and that, in obedience to this warrant, he and the other defendants, as his posse, entered upon the steamboat *Gen. Buell* and arrested Farris, and used only such force as was necessary to accomplish that arrest. The question as to the sufficiency of this plea was certified to this court, and it was held that the arrest of Farris upon the warrant from the state court was not an obstruction of the mail, or the retarding of the passage of a carrier of the mail, within the meaning of the act. In its opinion the court says: "All laws should receive a sensible construction. General terms should be so limited in their application as not to lead to injustice, oppression, or an absurd consequence. It will always, therefore, be presumed that the legislature intended exceptions to its language which would avoid results of this character. The reason of the law in such cases should prevail over its letter. The common sense of man approves the judgment mentioned by Puffendorf, that the Bolognian law which enacted 'that whoever drew blood in the streets should be punished with the utmost severity,' did not extend to the surgeon who opened the vein of a person that fell down in the street in a fit. The same common sense accepts the ruling, cited by Plowden, that the statute of 1 Edw. II., which enacts that a prisoner who breaks prison shall be guilty of felony, does not extend to a prisoner who breaks out when the prison is on fire, 'for he is not to be hanged because he would not stay to be burnt.' And we think that a like common sense will sanction the ruling we make, that the act of congress which punishes the obstruction or retarding of the passage of the mail, or of its carrier, does not apply to a case of temporary detention of the mail caused by the arrest of the carrier upon an indictment for murder." The following cases may also be cited: *Henry* v. *Tilson*, 17 Vt. 479; *Ryegate* v. *Wardsboro*, 30 Vt. 743; *Ex parte Ellis*, 11 Cal. 220; *Ingraham* v. *Speed*, 30 Miss. 410; *Jackson* v. *Collins*, 3 Cow. 89; *People* v. *Insurance Co.*, 15 Johns. 358; *Burch* v. *Newbury*, 10 N. Y. 374; *People* v. *Commissioners*, 95 N. Y. 554, 558; *People* v. *Lacombe*, 99 N. Y. 43, 49, 1 N. E. Rep. 599; *Chesapeake & Ohio Canal Co.* v. *Baltimore & Ohio R. Co.*, 4 Gill & J. 152; *Osgood* v. *Breed*, 12 Mass. 525, 530; *Wilbur* v. *Crane*, 13 Pick. 284; *Oates* v. *Bank*, 100 U. S. 239.

Among other things which may be considered in determining the intent of the legislature is the title of the act. We do not mean that it may be used to add to or take from the body of the statute, (*Hadden* v. *Collector*, 5 Wall. 107,) but it may help to interpret its meaning. In the case of *U.S.* v. *Fisher*, 2 Cranch, 358, 386, Chief Justice Marshall said: "On the influence which the title ought to have in construing the enacting clauses, much has been said, and yet it is not easy to discern the point of difference between the opposing counsel in this respect. Neither party contends that the title of an act can control plain words in the body of the statute; and neither denies that, taken with other parts, it may assist in removing ambiguities. Where the intent is plain, nothing is left to construction. Where the mind labors to discover the design of the legislature, it seizes everything from which aid can be derived; and in such case the title claims a degree of notice, and will have its due share of consideration." And in the case of *U.S.* v. *Palmer*, 3 Wheat. 610, 631, the same judge applied the doctrine in this way: "The words of the section are in terms of unlimited extent. The words 'any person or persons' are broad enough to comprehend every human being. But general words must not only be limited to cases within the jurisdiction of the state, but also to those objects to which the legislature intended to apply them. Did the legislature intend to apply these words to the subjects of a foreign power, who in a foreign ship may commit murder or robbery on the high seas? The title of an act cannot control its words, but may furnish some aid in showing what was in the mind of the legislature. The title of this act is, 'An act for the punishment of certain crimes against the United States.' It would seem that offenses against the United States, not offenses against the human race, were the crimes which the legislature intended by this law to punish."

It will be seen that words as general as those used in the first section of this act were by that decision limited, and the intent of congress with respect to the act was gathered partially, at least, from its title. Now, the title of this act is, "An act to prohibit the importation and migration of foreigners and aliens under contract or agreement to perform labor in the United States, its territories, and the District of Columbia." Obviously the thought expressed in this reaches only to the work of the manual laborer, as distinguished from that of the professional man. No one reading such a title would suppose that congress had in its mind any purpose of staying the coming into this country of ministers of the gospel, or, indeed, of any class whose toil is that of the brain. The common understanding of the terms "labor" and "laborers" does not include preaching and preachers, and it is to be assumed that words and phrases are used in their ordinary meaning. So whatever of light is thrown upon the statute by the language of the title indicates an exclusion from its penal provisions of all contracts for the employment of ministers, rectors, and pastors.

Again, another guide to the meaning of a statute is found in the evil which it is designed to remedy; and for this the court properly looks at contemporaneous events, the situation as it existed, and as it was pressed upon the attention of the legislative body. *U.S.* v. *Railroad Co.*, 91 U. S. 72, 79. The situation which called for this statute was briefly but fully stated by Mr. Justice Brown when, as district judge, he decided the case of *U.S.* v. *Craig*, 28 Fed. Rep. 795, 798: "The motives and history of the act are matters of common knowledge. It had become the practice for large capitalists in this country to contract with their agents abroad for the shipment of great numbers of an ignorant and servile class of foreign laborers, under contracts by which the employer agreed, upon the one hand, to prepay their passage, while, upon the other hand, the laborers agreed to work after their arrival for a certain time at a low rate of wages. The effect of this was to break down the labor market, and to reduce other laborers engaged in like occupations to the level of the assisted immigrant. The evil finally became so flagrant that an appeal was made to congress for relief by the passage of the act in question, the design of which was to raise the standard of foreign immigrants, and to discountenance the migration of those who had not sufficient means in their own hands, or those of their friends, to pay their passage."

It appears, also, from the petitions, and in the testimony presented before the committees of congress, that it was this cheap, unskilled labor which was making the trouble, and the influx of which congress sought to prevent. It was never suggested that we had in this country a surplus of brain toilers, and, least of all, that the market for the services of Christian ministers was depressed by foreign competition. Those were matters to which the attention of congress, or of the people, was not directed. So far, then, as the evil which was sought to be remedied interprets the statute, it also guides to an exclusion of this contract from the penalties of the act.

A singular circumstance, throwing light upon the intent of congress, is found in this extract from the report of the senate committee on education and labor, recommending the passage of the bill: "The general facts and considerations which induce the committee to recommend the passage of this bill are set forth in the report of the committee of the house. The committee report the bill back without amendment, although there are certain features thereof which might well be changed or modified, in the hope that the bill may not fail of passage during the present session. Especially would the committee have otherwise recommended amendments, substituting for the expression, 'labor and service,' whenever it occurs in the body of the bill, the words 'manual labor' or 'manual service,' as sufficiently broad to accomplish the purposes of the bill, and that such amendments would remove objections which a sharp and perhaps unfriendly criticism may urge to the proposed legislation. The committee, however, believing that the bill in its present form will be construed as including only those whose labor or service is manual in character, and being very desirous that the bill become a law before the adjournment, have reported the bill without change." Page 6059, *Congressional Record,* 48th Cong. And, referring back to the report of the committee of the house, there appears this language: "It seeks to restrain and prohibit the immigration or importation of laborers who would have never seen our shores but for the inducements and allurements of men whose only object is to obtain labor at the lowest possible rate, regardless of the social and material well-being of our own citizens, and regardless of the evil consequences which result to American laborers from such immigration. This class of immigrants care nothing about our institutions, and in many instances never even heard of them. They are men whose passage is paid by the importers. They come here under contract to labor for a certain number of years. They are ignorant of our social condition, and, that they may remain so, they are isolated and prevented from coming into contact with Americans. They are generally from the lowest social stratum, and live upon the coarsest food, and in hovels of a character before unknown to American workmen. They, as a rule, do not become citizens, and are certainly not a desirable acquisition to the body politic. The inevitable tendency of their presence among us is to degrade American labor, and to reduce it to the level of the imported pauper labor." Page 5359, *Congressional Record,* 48th Cong.

We find, therefore, that the title of the act, the evil which was intended to be remedied, the circumstances surrounding the appeal to congress, the reports of the committee of each house, all concur in affirming that the intent of congress was simply to stay the influx of this cheap, unskilled labor.

But, beyond all these matters, no purpose of action against religion can be imputed to any legislation, state or national, because this is a religious people. This is historically true. From the discovery of this continent to the present hour, there is a single voice making this affirmation. The commission to Christopher Columbus, prior to his sail westward, is from "Ferdinand and Isabella, by the grace of God, king and queen of Castile," etc., and recites that "it is hoped that by God's assistance some of the continents and islands in the ocean will be discovered," etc. The first colonial grant, that made to Sir Walter Raleigh in 1584, was from "Elizabeth, by the grace of God, of England, Fraunce, and Ireland, queene, defender of the faith," etc.; and the grant authorizing him to enact statutes of the government of the proposed colony provided that "they be not against the true Christian faith nowe professed in the Church of England." The first charter of Virginia, granted by King James I in 1606, after reciting the application of certain parties for a charter, commenced the grant in these words: "We, greatly commending, and graciously accepting of, their Desires for the Furtherance of so noble a Work, which may, by the Providence of Almighty God, hereafter tend to the Glory of His Divine Majesty, in propagating of Christian Religion to such People, as yet live in Darkness and miserable Ignorance of the true Knowledge and Worship of God, and may in time bring the Infidels and Savages, living in those parts, to human Civility, and to a settled and quiet Government; DO, by these our Letters-Patents, graciously accept of, and agree to, their humble and well-intentioned Desires."

Language of similar import may be found in the subsequent charters of that colony from the same king, in 1609 and 1611; and the same is true of the various charters granted to the other colonies. In language more or less emphatic is the establishment of the Christian religion declared to be one of the purposes of the grant. The celebrated compact made by the pilgrims in the *Mayflower*, 1620, recites: "Having undertaken for the Glory of God, and Advancement of the Christian Faith, and the Honour of our King and Country, a Voyage to plant the first Colony in the northern Parts of Virginia; Do by these Presents, solemnly and mutually, in the Presence of God and one another, covenant and combine ourselves together into a civil Body Politick, for our better Ordering and Preservation, and Furtherance of the Ends aforesaid."

The fundamental orders of Connecticut, under which a provisional government was instituted in 1638–39, commence with this declaration: "Forasmuch as it hath pleased the Allmighty God by the wise disposition of his diuyne pruidence so to order and dispose of things that we the Inhabitants and Residents of Windsor, Hartford, and Wethersfield are now cohabiting and dwelling in and vppon the River of Conectecotte and the Lands thereunto adioyneing; And well knowing where a people are gathered together the word of God requires that to mayntayne the peace and union of such a people there should be an orderly and decent Gouerment established according to God, to order and dispose of tho affayres of the people at all seasons as occation shall require; doe therefore assotiate and conioyne our sclues to be as one Publike State or Commonwelth; and doe, for our selues and our Successors and such as shall be adioyned to vs att any tyme hereafter, enter into Combination and Confederation togather, to mayntayne and presearue the liberty and purity of the gospell of our Lord Jesus wch we now p^rfesse, as also the disciplyne of the Churches, wch according to the truth of the said gospell is now practised amongst vs."

In the charter of privileges granted by William Penn to the province of Pennsylvania, in 1701, it is recited: "Because no People can be truly happy, though under the greatest Enjoyment of Civil Liberties, if abridged of the Freedom of their Consciences, as to their Religious Profession and Worship; And Almighty God being the only Lord of Conscience, Father of Lights and Spirits; and the Author as well as Object of all divine Knowledge, Faith, and Worship, who only doth enlighten the Minds, and persuade and convince the Understandings of People, I do hereby grant and declare," etc.

Coming nearer to the present time, the Declaration of Independence recognizes the presence of the Divine in human affairs in these words: "We hold these truths to be self-evident, that all men are created equal, that they are endowed by their Creator with certain unalienable Rights, that among these are Life, Liberty and the pursuit of Happiness." "We, therefore, the Representatives of the united States of America, in General Congress, Assembled, appealing to the Supreme Judge of the world for the rectitude of our intentions, do, in the Name and by Authority of the good People of these Colonies, solemnly publish and declare," etc.; "And for the support of this Declaration, with a firm reliance on the Protection of Divine Providence, we mutually pledge to each other our Lives, our Fortunes, and our sacred Honor."

If we examine the constitutions of the various states, we find in them a constant recognition of religious obligations. Every constitution of every one of the forty-four states contains language which, either directly or by clear implication, recognizes a profound reverence for religion, and an assumption that its influence in all human affairs is essential to the well-being of the community. This recognition may be in the preamble, such as is found in the constitution of Illinois, 1870: "We, the people of the state of Illinois, grateful to Almighty God for the civil, political, and religious liberty which He hath so long permitted us to enjoy, and looking to Him for a blessing upon our endeavors to secure and transmit the same unimpaired to succeeding generations," etc.

It may be only in the familiar requisition that all officers shall take an oath closing with the declaration, "so help me God." It may be in clauses like that of the constitution of Indiana, 1816, art. XI, section 4: "The manner of administering an oath or affirmation shall be such as is most consistent with the conscience of the deponent, and shall be esteemed the most solemn appeal to God." Or in provisions such as are found in articles 36 and 37 of the declaration of the rights of the constitution of Maryland, (1867): "That, as it is the duty of every man to worship God in such manner as he thinks most acceptable to Him, all persons are equally entitled to protection in their religious liberty: wherefore, no person ought, by any law, to be molested in his person or estate on account of his religious persuasion or profession, or for his religious practice, unless, under the color of religion, he shall disturb the good order, peace, or safety of the state, or shall infringe the laws of morality, or injure others in their natural, civil, or religious rights; nor ought any person to be compelled to frequent or maintain or contribute, unless on contract, to maintain any place of worship or any ministry; nor shall any person, otherwise competent, be deemed incompetent as a witness or juror on account of his religious belief: provided, he believes in the existence of God, and that, under his dispensation, such person will be held morally accountable for his acts, and be rewarded or punished therefor, either in this world or the world to come. That no religious test ought ever to be required as a qualification for any office or profit or trust in this state, other than a declaration of belief in the existence of God; nor shall the legislature prescribe any other oath of office than the oath prescribed by this constitution." Or like that in articles 2 and 3 of part 1 of the constitution of Massachusetts, (1780:) "It is the right as well as the duty of all men in society publicly, and at stated seasons, to worship the Supreme Being, the Great Creator and Preserver of the universe. . . . As the happiness of a people and the good order and preservation of civil government essentially depend upon piety, religion, and morality, and as these cannot be generally diffused through a community but by the institution of the public worship of God and of public instructions in piety, religion, and morality: Therefore, to promote their happiness, and to secure the good order and preservation of their government, the people of this commonwealth have a right to invest their legislature with power to authorize and require, and the legislature shall, from time to time, authorize and require, the several towns, parishes, precincts, and other bodies politic or religious societies to make suitable provision, at their own expense, for the institution of the public worship of God and for the support and maintenance of public Protestant teachers of piety, religion

and morality, in all cases where such provisions shall not be made voluntar-
ily." Or, as in sections 5 and 14 of article 7 of the constitution of Mississippi,
(1832:) "No person who denies the being of a God, or a future state of rewards and punishments, shall hold any office in the civil department of this
state. . . . Religion, morality, and knowledge being necessary to good government, the preservation of liberty, and the happiness of mankind, schools,
and the means of education, shall forever be encouraged in this state." Or by
article 22 of the constitution of Delaware, (1776,) which required all officers,
besides an oath of allegiance, to make and subscribe the following declaration: "I, A. B., do profess faith in God the Father, and in Jesus Christ His
only Son, and in the Holy Ghost, one God, blessed for evermore; and I do
acknowledge the Holy Scriptures of the Old and New Testament to be given
by divine inspiration."

Even the Constitution of the United States, which is supposed to have
little touch upon the private life of the individual, contains in the first amendment a declaration common to the constitutions of all the states, as follows:
"Congress shall make no law respecting an establishment of religion, or prohibiting the free exercise thereof," etc.,— and also provides in article 1, section 7, (a provision common to many constitutions,) that the executive shall
have ten days (Sundays excepted) within which to determine whether he
will approve or veto a bill.

There is no dissonance in these declarations. There is a universal language pervading them all, having one meaning. They affirm and reaffirm
that this is a religious nation. These are not individual sayings, declarations
of private persons. They are organic utterances. They speak the voice of the
entire people. While because of a general recognition of this truth the question has seldom been presented to the courts, yet we find that in *Updegraph*
v. *Comm.*, 11 Serg. & R. 394, 400, it was decided that, "Christianity, general
Christianity, is, and always has been, a part of the common law of Pennsylvania; . . . not Christianity with an established church and tithes and spiritual courts, but Christianity with liberty of conscience to all men." And in
People v. *Ruggles,* 8 Johns. 290, 294, 295, Chancellor Kent, the great commentator on American law, speaking as chief justice of the supreme court of
New York, said: "The people of this state, in common with the people of this
country, profess the general doctrines of Christianity as the rule of their

faith and practice; and to scandalize the author of those doctrines is not
only, in a religious point of view, extremely impious, but, even in respect to
the obligations due to society, is a gross violation of decency and good order.
. . . The free, equal, and undisturbed enjoyment of religious opinion, whatever it may be, and free and decent discussions on any religious subject, is
granted and secured; but to revile, with malicious and blasphemous contempt, the religion professed by almost the whole community is an abuse of
that right. Nor are we bound by any expressions in the Constitution, as
some have strangely supposed, either not to punish at all, or to punish indis-
criminately the like attacks upon the religion of Mahomet or of the Grand
Lama; and for this plain reason that the case assumes that we are a Christian people, and the morality of the country is deeply ingrafted upon Christianity, and not upon the doctrines or worship of those impostors." And in
the famous case of *Vidal* v. *Girard's Ex'rs,* 2 How. 127, 198, this court, while
sustaining the will of Mr. Girard, with its provisions for the creation of a
college into which no minister should be permitted to enter, observed: "it is
also said, and truly, that the Christian religion is a part of the common law
of Pennsylvania."

If we pass beyond these matters to a view of American life, as expressed
by its laws, its business, its customs, and its society, we find everywhere a
clear recognition of the same truth. Among other matters note the following: The form of oath universally prevailing, concluding with an appeal to
the Almighty; the custom of opening sessions of all deliberative bodies and
most conventions with prayer; the prefatory words of all wills, "In the name
of God, amen;" the laws respecting the observance of the Sabbath, with the
general cessation of all secular business, and the closing of courts, legisla-
tures, and other similar public assemblies on that day; the churches and
church organizations which abound in every city, town, and hamlet; the
multitude of charitable organizations existing everywhere under Christian
auspices; the gigantic missionary associations, with general support, and
aiming to establish Christian missions in every quarter of the globe. These
and many other matters which might be noticed, add a volume of unofficial
declarations to the mass of organic utterances that **this is a Christian
nation**. In the face of all these, shall it be believed that a congress of the
United States intended to make it a misdemeanor for a church of this coun-

try to contract for the services of a Christian minister residing in another nation?

Suppose, in the congress that passed this act, some member had offered a bill which in terms declared that, if any Roman Catholic church in this country should contract with Cardinal Manning to come to this country, and enter into its service as pastor and priest, or any Episcopal church should enter into a like contract with Canon Farrar, or any Baptist church should make similar arrangements with Rev. Mr. Spurgeon, or any Jewish synagogue with some eminent rabbi, such contract should be adjudged unlawful and void, and the church making it be subject to prosecution and punishment. Can it be believed that it would have received a minute of approving thought or a single vote? Yet it is contended that such was, in effect, the meaning of this statute. The construction invoked cannot be accepted as correct. It is a case where there was presented a definite evil, in view of which the legislature used general terms with the purpose of reaching all phases of that evil; and thereafter, unexpectedly, it is developed that the general language thus employed is broad enough to reach cases and acts which the whole history and life of the country affirm could not have been intentionally legislated against. It is the duty of the courts, under those circumstances, to say that, however broad the language of the statute may be, the act, although within the letter, is not with the intention of the legislature, and therefore cannot be within the statute.

The judgment will be reversed, and the case
remanded for further proceedings in accordance with the opinion.

Election Sermon

Jesus Christ the true King and Head of Government

*A sermon preached before the Assembly of the State of Vermont,
on the day of their first election, March 12, 1778, at Windsor
by Peter Powers, pastor of the Church in Newbury*

And Jesus came and spake unto them saying, All power is given unto me in
heaven and in earth.

—Matthew 28:18

The King of Kings and Lord of Lords is the divine speaker in these great
words. And how august and glorious he appears, as the anointed of the Father, on his mediatorial Throne! His unlimited sovereignty and absolute dominion, in and over all things, is clearly asserted.

He, who was by nature the supreme and mighty God, was pleased to
take the form of a servant and the fashion of man, that he might suffer the
demerit of our sins. He humbled himself and became obedient unto death,
even the death of the Cross, for which God the father *hath highly exalted
him, and given him a name above every name, that at the name of Jesus every
knee should bow—and that every tongue should confess that Jesus Christ is
Lord* [Phil. 2:6–11].

Accordingly, our Lord, after his resurrection, appeared in the clearer
and more bright effulgence of His Deity. In his estate of humiliation he did
not lay aside his divinity, but shrouded the glorious appearance of it with the
weakness of human flesh. Yet, in the mean time, how frequently did the sun
break forth through those clouds, in the wonderful miracles he wrought?
But now, having finished transgression in his expiatory sacrifice, and
risen triumphant over death and hell; as the due reward of his sufferings, *he*

has power over all flesh, and all power in heaven and earth given unto him.

Hence, we have the most natural observation from the Text.

Jesus Christ is the head and fountain of all power.

This, by divine help, I shall endeavor to discuss by shewing,

I.   What is intended by power, and all power.

II.   How Jesus Christ is the head and fountain of all power.

III.   Make application.

I. I am to shew what may be here intended by power, or all power in heaven and earth.

Power is a word of large and extensive sense, especially here, where our Lord declares it to be *all power* in heaven and in earth. So that we may well conceive that there is no kind of power, but it is, in some just sense, his.

Power signifies both *right* and *ability* to perform any thing.

There is the power of strength, and the power of authority and dominion. And there is divine power, and the power of creatures. Among men there is civil, military, and ecclesiastical power; but Jesus Christ is the great head and fountain of all.

Divine power is infinite, and bounded by nothing but the [absolute?] will and pleasure of the great supreme. Hence this title is assumed by God, and abundantly attributed to him with infinite propriety, THE ALMIGHTY. *I am the Almighty God* [Gen. 17:1]. *I know, says Job, that thou canst do everything* [Job 42:2]. Whatever God wills to do, he does with infinite pleasure. His almighty *Fiat* gives immediate existence to things, and nothing can resist. It equally creates, preserves, and governs all things. How marvelous and surprising the all-enlivening agency of the divine power, in every successful moment, in every infinite variety and multiplicity of existencies in the wide extended creation? And thus says our Lord, *My Father worketh hitherto, and I work* [John 5:17].

But divine power is not only manifested in the creation, conservation, and subornation of all things, but most gloriously, in the redemption and salvation of mankind sinners by Jesus Christ, who therefore says, *All power is given unto me, in heaven and in earth.* It was a work of almighty power, as well as of infinite grace, to make satisfaction for our sins: and, at the same time, to make a complete conquest of the rebellious power of infernal darkness. [On] the cross of our great Lord spoiled principalities and powers.

The work of effectual calling is a work of almighty power, when our Lord raises the dead sinner from his long sleep and death in sin, to a new and divine life, and strengthens him to faith and calling upon God. Therefore we read, *You hath he quickened, who were dead in trespasses and sins* [Eph. 2:1]. *The hour is coming, and now is, when the dead shall hear the voice of the son of God; and they that hear shalt live* [John 5:25]. *Who believe according to the working of his mighty power, which he wrought in Christ when he raised him from the dead* [Eph. 1:19–20].

Moreover, the guardianship and protection of the church, admist all the wickedness of their own hearts, men and devils; and of every danger, through this world, to the heavenly kingdom, is a work of powerful grace.

But there is not only the power of almightiness in God, but also of *Authority* and *Dominion*. *Dominion and fear are with him.* He is the great Lord and lawgiver of the universe. Being God [creator] and preserver, he has a most just right to give law to, and govern all his creatures.

In infinite wisdom, the creator fixed a law of nature to every species of beings animate and inanimate. And according to that law is the system governed. Nature, or its fixed laws, is nothing without him who is the God of nature. He manages the ordinances of heaven agreeably to his wise constitution. The wide field of nature in this lower world, obeys his sovereign orders, and sets a beautiful example of perfect submission to men, originally appointed its ruler, made but a little lower than the angels, and crowned with glory and honour.

Law was given to man. The original law our Maker gave us, commonly called the *law of nature,* was not a blind law of instinct, but *the eternal rule of righteousness,* the moral law, agreeably to the nature of the divine perfections. The spirit of this law was written on the heart of innocent man, *for in the image of God made he them;* and the great Creator positively enjoined his punctual obedience. Man is still bound by the same authority; and the heaven and earth shall sooner pass away than one jot or tittle of the law shall fail, or be dispensed with. *Jehovah* will maintain his authority over his reasonable creatures, be the consequences what it will to them.

Had not man broken the law of his Creation it would have been the security of his happiness, but being broken, its sanction must take place without an equal reparation be made, for God is unchangeable. Blessed be his name for our divine surety Jesus Christ.

Great is the authority of God. He reigns in heaven above and governs the myriads of angelic hosts and glorified saints at his pleasure. And unspeakably happy are they under his government. He reigns upon earth, and nothing makes any subject unhappy or miserable under his dominion, but rebellion and high treason against his majesty.

I proceed to say,

There is the power of creatures. Angels excel in strength, and they have principality and dominion. Hence we read of thrones, dominions, principalities and powers in heavenly places [Eph. 3:10; Col. 1:16].

And there is power and authority among men. The strength of man is final and limited, and so is his authority. But authority among mankind is absolutely reasonable and necessary.

All men, indeed, are by nature equal: and all have, most certainly, an equal right to freedom and liberty by the great law of nature. No man or number of men, *has* or *can* have a right to infringe the natural rights, liberties of privileges of others: or to dominion or government over any one, but by his free consent personally, or by his legal representative, God having created the human species upon a level.

But then, we are to consider that the alwise Creator has laid a foundation for society in the creation of man. It was not good for man to be alone. God therefore made, and instituted the society of man and wife, which laid the foundation for larger societies from one degree and rise to another, until it came to nations, kingdoms or common wealths. Therefore when men, after their apostasy, multiplied upon the face of the earth, it was necessary to form into political and civil society, and to have rules and laws for their protection, and safety; and to appoint guardians of the same, else the lives and property of men could not be safe from the outrages of the wicked, who paid no regard to any law, but of sin and corrupt nature. So that the true original end of civil government was, the safety and happiness of the people; that every man, so far as possible, might enjoy his immunities and privileges in peaceable and quiet possession.

We read, *The powers that be are ordained of God.* But for what purpose?

He, namely the civil magistrate, *is the minister of God to thee for good; but if thou do that which is evil, be afraid, for he beareth not the sword in vain: for he is the minister of God, a revenger to execute wrath upon him that doeth evil* (Rom. 8:1–4). And again we are told, *The law is not made for a righteous man, but for the lawless and disobedient, for the ungodly and for sinners, for unholy and prophane, for murderers of fathers and murderers of mothers, for man-flayers, for whoremongers, for them that defile themselves with mankind, for stealers, for liars, for perjured persons, and if there be any other thing that is contrary to sound doctrine* [1 Tim. 1:9–10].

Whatever different forms of government have been set up, among all nations since the flood, they have been, professedly, set up with these views. Even the worst of tyrants have openly professed the same, although their practice has been a palpable contradiction to them. And the most barbarous heathen nations have found it necessary to have established rules and customary laws strictly observed for the punishment of vice, and for the safety of life, and preservation of property.

The people, under God, are the fountain of all authority among men. Even in the land of Palestine, where their government was a Theocracy and their God was their King, and raised up by their Judges and Kings by an extraordinary call, yet they did not enter upon government without the people's consent and appointment. Saul and David were particularly pointed out by God, and anointed by special direction to Samuel the prophet. Yet, without, and until the people's acceptance, they meddled not with any affair of government.

The people of any nation, country, or community, have an undoubted right to set up such form of government as they judge will most effectually secure their fates, prosperity and happiness: and to change and alter it, as they shall find requisite for the good ends of Government.

And every ruler is, or ought to be, appointed by the people, and accountable to them. And for any officer to make his own private emolument, or personal honor his aim, is at once to deviate from the design of his institution, and to enter upon the first stages of tyranny. The public good should ever be the highest aim, next to God and his own soul, of every one constituted to any office in the State. But then,

It is necessary that the constitution be well framed, and suitably adapted, not only to the genius of the people, but agreeably to the great law of nature. And divine revelation, which gives us the most perfect rules for the conduct of mankind, in every nation and condition of civil and religious life, should be received, as a perfect standard, in the framing of all human laws. *The law of the Lord is perfect.* Yet as we are never to look for another theocracy since the Jewish is sealed, and their laws were fitted to such a state, it is necessary that laws be made in every civil State, to answer the necessities and conveniences of the subject.

And not only is it necessary to the well being and happiness of every State, that there be a good constitution, and good laws agreeably thereto, but good rulers, appointed by the people, for the due execution of them. In this case Jethro's counsel to Moses is worthy of our observation. *Moreover thou shalt choose out of all the people, able men, such as fear God, men of truth, hating covetousness, and place such over them* [Exod. 18:21]. Rulers are over the people in their office, but their power is limited by the constitution: and whenever they abuse it, the people have right to a redress of their greivances; and to depose them from their offices.

Officers should be faithful, and be supported by the people, for this is the mind of God. *Wherefore ye must needs be subject, not only for wrath, but also for conscience sake. For, this cause pay ye tribute also: for they are God's ministers attending continually upon this very thing* [Rom. 13:5–6]. Faithful rulers have, in proportion, a great weight, the weight of the State lying upon them: and they need much wisdom and fortitude that they may do worthily for God and his people.

Every one should be content with his place and labor to fill his station with honor to himself and constituents. When once men are uneasy to act within their own spheres, and covet to rise to higher preferments of honor or profit; when they are proud, haughty and hasty; when they treat their inferiors with scorn and contempt; when they wink and connive at vice, or are vicious themselves, they shew plainly that they are unfit to be trusted by the freemen of the State, and unworthy of their good regards. If such men are promoted, the constitution is injured, and the laws violated with impunity. Oppression, despotism and tyranny will soon get off their shackles and presently begin to lift up their *Hydra heads* and, with wide strides, like hideous monsters over the extended country. Surely the people cannot well be too cautious who they promote to offices. As good rulers are a great blessing to people, and highly deserving of their respect; so, on the other hand, bad rulers are a fore judgment, and deserve the frowns of the public.

Again, military power is also of God, and ordained for the defense of the civil, and must ever by subject to it, and regulated by it. But this I must pass over.

Once more here, ecclesiastical power is wholly of a spiritual nature, and no ways connected with either civil or military power. Christ's *kingdom is not of this world*, not of a worldly nature. The constitution is spiritual, *the covenant of grace*. The laws are spiritual, and the ordinances of a spiritual nature, given us in the word of truth, the great statutes of heaven; and the punishments are spiritual, being the sentences of Christ's mouth, who is the only king, Lord and law-giver of his church, and pronounced against offenders in his name, by his ministers. Therefore the civil magistrate has nothing to do with this government. Only the civil rights, privileges and properties of the church are to be secured and defended by the civil powers.

Passing other denominations of power, I proceed to the second general head of our discourse.

II. To show how Jesus Christ is the head and fountain of all power. Here I would say,

1. Jesus Christ is the head and fountain, the author and bestower of all authority as he is *by nature God*. He is God over all, blessed forevermore. For, let us consider.

He is the creator of all things, *By him* says St. Paul, *were all things created that are in heaven, and that are in earth, visible and invisible, whether they be thrones, dominions, principalities, or powers, all things were created by him and for him.* (a) *the world was made by him* [Col. 1:16]. (b) And the father says to him, *Thou Lord in the beginning hast laid the foundations of the earth, and the heavens are the works of thine hands* [John 1:10].

(c) [Heb. 1:10] MOREOVER, Jesus Christ is the immediate *upholder, preserver* and *governor* of all worlds. And thus we read of him, *And upholding all things by the word of his power.* (d) *And by him all things consist* [Heb. 1:3]. (e) *Yea, he is head over all things* [Col. 1:17]. (f) *The government is upon his shoulder, and he is the mighty God, the everlasting Father,* or the father of eternity. (g) And when he *tabernacled in the flesh and dwelt among*

us he wrought many surprising miracles by his own power and authority.—
The names and titles of Deity are clearly ascribed to him, with all the divine
attributes and perfections, as Eternity, Immutability, Omniscience, Omni-
presence, Omnipotence, and Absolute Supremacy.

Divine worship is given to him by the command of God, who will not
give his glory to another: even the eternal Father says, *Let all the angels of
God worship him.*

(h) [Heb. 1:6] Finally our Lord will raise the dead, bring every work into
Judgment, with every secret thing, and judge the quick and the dead according to their works. Surely these things argue infinite Deity so that we may,
without doubt, determine that our Lord is absolute God, and therefore the
natural and original head of all power and authority.

2. Jesus Christ is the head and fountain of all authority and power in
his *mediatorial capacity*. Jesus Christ, as mediator, has received a very extensive commission. The Father has constituted him to *be heard over all
things.* He that stood as a criminal in Pilate's bar, who was unjustly tried,
condemned and inhumanly executed by the treasonous leaders as the meri-
torious reward of his sufferings, is advanced to the imperial crown of the
universe: Angels, principalities, and powers are made subject unto him. All
things are put under him.

This is by a special appointment of the Father, to Saint Paul, *Wherefore
God also hath highly exalted him and given him a name which is above every
name* [Phil. 2:9]. And *we see Jesus who was made a little lower than the
angels, for the suffering of death, crowned with glory and honor* [Heb. 2:9]
God hath set him at his own right hand, exalted him in the highest degree,
with the highest honors. Therefore has he given all the angels command to
worship and obey the Son as Mediator, being, in that capacity, exalted as
head over them.

All worlds are subject unto our Lord as God, Creator, but now they are
subject unto him in his mediatorial capacity, his commission extending to
universal dominion. So he is Lord of heaven and earth, and has the keys of
death and hell, yea, and of heaven too; for the Father has given him *power
over all flesh, that he should give eternal life to as many as he has given him*
[John 17:2].

Therefore, not only is Jesus Christ king of angels, having the glorious host of those morning stars perfectly obsequious to his sovereign authority, but *he is the church's King*. Not only is he the prophet and priest of his people, but also their great sovereign. He is their only Lord and lawgiver, and they have no other head. The church has no inferior and subordinate heads. Officers he has to administer the word and sacraments to her, as also her censures and admonitions to offenders, according to the mind of Christ. In the church there is the authority of offices for edification and assistance in government, but Jesus Christ is *head over all things unto the church* [Eph. 1:22]. Agreeably the Father says, *I have set my king upon my holy hill of Zion* [Ps. 2:6].

And our Lord not only exercises his kingly office in giving law to, and ruling over his church, but also in conquering all her internal opposition to him, subduing her corruptions, giving ruling, and exercising grace, and in refraining and conquering all her spiritual and temporal enemies, and in effectually guarding and defending her through life and death, unto glory. Once more, Jesus Christ is King of all the earth. He is the great prince of the kings of the earth. Therefore we read, *God reigneth over the heathen, and God is king of all the earth* [Ps. 17:7–8]. And he has this title, *King of kings and Lord of lords* [Rev. 19:16]. He is also represented as standing with one foot on the earth and the other on the sea, denoting his dominion over earth and sea.

Question. What sort of dominion has Christ over the world?

I answer, PROVIDENTIAL. The government of Christ over the heathen, and so also, over all mankind, is a providential government. Jesus Christ is exalted to the seat of absolute and universal dominion in providence. He wisely and secretly, according to his own sovereign pleasure, guides all the springs of action, in all kingdoms and nations through the whole world. Thrones, dominions, principalities and powers are made subject unto him in providence.

Wicked men universally oppose and resist our Lord's revealed will, and refuse submission to his laws. *They break his bands asunder, and cast away his cords.* And all his grace, brought them in the gospel, is slighted, despised, and condemned by them. They will not have him reign in their hearts, but he reigns over them in providence. He is King in providence ordering all events. It is by his permissive will that Satan rages and triumphs among pagans, mahometans, papists, jews, and multitudes of professed protestants. All the arbitrary tyranny and most barbarous cruelties exercised in all parts of the world, are by his permission. All the different forts and species of governments in the world, and all the rulers, good and bad, are set up by his providential will. Saul and David, Josiah and Nebuchadnezzar are witness of both.

Kings and princes receive their kingdoms and territories, and all their power of jurisdiction from Christ, and so does every officer civil or military, although it be through the hands of the people. Therefore says he, *By me all kings reign and princes decree justice; by me princes rule and nobles, even all the judges of the earth.* But truly it may be said of many of them, as God did to Cyrus, *I girded thee, though thou hast not known me* [Isa. 32].

As *all judgments is committed to the Son,* in his mediatorial capacity, *and the Father judges no man,* for he manages all the affairs of the world, ruling and reigning over, and disposing of all nations and countries, and every person among them, and every thing concerning them, according to his sovereign pleasure. He is that God who *standeth in the congregation of the mighty,* and *judgeth among the gods.* The world of nature is in his hands. The natural and moral system is by and under him. Therefore says he, *I form the light, and create darkness; I make peace, and create evil: I the Lord do all these things* [Isa. 14]. Hence, it is evident that a great and infinite good shall be brought out of all the evils, both moral and penal, permitted or suffered in the world. Jesus reigns universal sovereign. I now proceed to the IMPROVEMENT.

IMPROVEMENT

And this shall be assayed in two uses.

I. Use of information and instruction. And from what we have heard of God's Almightiness we may infer,

1. The safety and security of all that have taken sanctuary under the divine wings. God is able to defend them, and will surely do it, for he has promised saying, *He shall cover thee with his feathers, and under his wings shall thou trust; his truth shall be thy shield and buckler* [Ps. 91:4–16]. Chastisement they shall have, but this is not to be deemed evil, but good for them. They shall have safety in all their troubles; safety in the greatest dan-

gers, and in death itself. The almighty arm will defend them from the powers of darkness, confront and subdue all opposition to their best good, and
guard them to glory, beyond the reach of all enemies.

2. We infer the inexpressible, infinite danger and most exquisite misery
of God's enemies. Whatever their characters or stations, their danger is infinite. *Thine hand shall find out all thine enemies; thy right hand shall find
out those that hate thee. Thou shalt make them as a fiery oven in the time of
thine anger. The Lord shalt swallow them up in his wrath, and the fire shall
devour them* [Ps. 21:8–9]. They that oppose Christ's laws and government in
the world; that refute allegiance to him; that break his laws and abuse his
grace, and continue in their groundless unbelief, let them be high or low,
rich or poor, *He shalt break them with a rod of iron, He shalt dash them in
pieces like a potter's vessel* [Ps. 2:2,9]. Surely the following counsel is of infinite importance. *Be wise now therefore, O ye kings, be instructed ye judges of
the earth. Serve the Lord with fear, and rejoice with trembling. Kiss the son,
lest he be angry, and ye perish from the way when his wrath is kindled but a
little. Blessed are all they that put their truth in him.*

O what an Almighty arm is lifted up over the impious hardened rebels
against heaven! And *can thine heart endure, and can thy hands be strong in
the day that God shall deal with thee?* You may go on a little while, perhaps,
in your mad defiance of our maker and your judge, and spurn at all the grace
tendered you, most freely and plentifully, in the blessed gospel, and take
your course, but *in due time your foot shall slide.* Methinks I see crowns and
scepters thrown away as vile refuse; and all the glittering glory of titles,
honors, riches, and earthly profits condemned as the mire in the streets.
*The kings of the earth, and the great men, and the rich men, and the chief of
captains, and the mighty men, every bond man, and every free man hiding
themselves in the dens, and the rocks of the mountains, saying to the mountains and rocks, fall on us and hide us from the face of him that sitteth on the
throne, and from the wrath of the Lamb: for the great day of his wrath is
come, and who shall be able to stand?* Can we now refrain thinking of those
words of our blessed Saviour, *What shall it profit a man if he shall gain the
whole world, and lose his own soul?* A portion in Christ is worth more than
the world. O that great men and rich men would not look upon themselves
above religion! *Hath thou an arm like God? Or canst thou thunder with a*

voice like him? It is very absurd for a glittering worm to vaunt itself as above its fellow worms when nature is the same, and as liable and as easy to be crushed to death?

Secondly, from what has been offered on the divine authority, we infer,

1. That it is most reasonable and just. It is the authority of God our maker, of Christ our God and Redeemer. And authority over all is a natural and necessary prerogative of the Deity. Nothing can be more reasonable than that the creator should be absolute proprietor of his creatures; and that he should give them laws and govern them to the greatest and best end, his own glory. And impossible it is for him to err. His will must be good, for his will is not only good, but his understanding infinite. Therefore his authority is most reasonable and just.

2. We infer that submission to the divine government is our duty. And an imperfect submission and obedience is far from the thing required. An imperfect obodience to the laws of the state, would rather be termed rebellion, or disobedience by the rulers. Though a man should keep the laws of the state in a thousand instances, and violate them willfully in one, he would be deemed guilty, and dealt with as a law-breaker. And so divine inspiration argues, *Whoever shall keep the whole law, and yet offend in one point is guilty of all, for he that said do not commit adultery, said also, do not kill. Now if thou commit no adultery, yet if thou kill, thou art become a transgressor of the law* [Jam. 2:10–11].

Surely, if God be infinite and his law perfect, and we read expressly that *the law of the Lord is perfect* [Ps. 19:7] then a perfect submission and obedience is our duty; and also a continuance therein, for it is written, *cursed is every one that continueth not in all things which are written in the book of the law to do them* [Gal. 3:10]. Oh, if Christ had not most perfectly obeyed for us, the curse would have been our portion forever: But blessed be God, he has become obedient unto death for us, that whosoever believeth in him should receive remission of sins, and be freely justified and saved. Yet the believers in Jesus must be careful to maintain good works. Indeed the law is not a covenant of works for the believer, but a perfect rule of all holy living unto God. But I pass on to say,

Thirdly, from what we have heard of authority among men, we learn,

1. That the authority from which is founded on the law of nature, and

agreeably to divine revelation, is the authority of God, and the only authority to be obeyed, all other power and authority being tyranny. True, many
nations have set a constitution of government, which has, in many things,
been excellent, and many of their laws have been well adapted to the necessities of the state. The Romans seemed to have excelled most others, while
they remained a Common Wealth. But many encroachments were made upon
the rights of the subject among them; and finally that empire has undergone
seven or eight different forms of government. We indeed find that under one
of the worst of those forms, namely, their emperors, Saint Paul directs Christians to be subjects [Rom. 8:1]. But we are not to suppose any are bound to
be subject to any law or government, in any article against the rights of
conscience. The holy martyrs of Jesus have ever submitted to the civil laws
of the government they lived under, acknowledging their bodies and estates
belonged to the king, or emperor, but their consciences they held free.

It is observable, that toleration to those of a different religion from the
state-religion, was but little considered as a matter of right, in but few countries: so that spiritual tyranny and intolerance generally prevailed in the
world from age to age. And even in England, after they became professed
protestants, they were no less severe against dissenters than the old pagans
and papists. And, as to civil liberty, in the best regulated states, kingdoms
and common wealths, there ever was a high degree of tyranny practiced
against the subject.

England has been one of the most famous countries for civil liberty. The
people, in almost every age, seemed to have an abhorrence for despotism,
and have shewn an uncommon zeal to secure and establish their privileges.
Yet, notwithstanding their great *Charter*, and the established laws of the
nation, almost every reign has been stained with more or less acts of tyranny. And, in many reigns, what scenes of the most savage barbarities have
been carried on, to the eternal infamy of the Henry and Stuart lines? In the
mean time how have the pulpits run with the stupid doctrine of *the Lord's
anointed* and *passive obedience* and *non-resistance?* The nation groaned under the weight of oppression and arbitrary domination. Nothing could content the more than brutish tyrants but the absolute destruction and waste
of law, every privilege, and the lives and fortunes of the subject. Happy revolution in 1688. But how has the old tyranny risen out of its grave, and made

a most formidable attack upon the subject in the present arbitrary reign? This country, sensible of the vast importance of its privileges, has thrown off the yoke, and nobly taken up arms in its own defense, determined to be free, or die in the virtuous cause, the great cause of heaven and earth. In dependence on the almighty Jehovah, we may expect complete deliverance, and see this infant country a seat of justice, religion and liberty.

Unhappy it would be, if the bad government we have been under should be a means of the people's neglecting a good government. Rather let it engage them the more carefully to establish, maintain and submit to good government. But in this sinful world, we cannot expect a permanent state of peace, liberty, and prosperity. Such is the corruption, pride and avarice of fallen man, that it makes him like the *troubled sea when it cannot rest.* And the first temptation, *ye shall be as gods,* is very apt to prevail, especially in unsanctified men. Internal disputes may embroil the whole land in a scene of disorder, confusion and misery. Or sensuality, luxury and dissipation swallow up all our virtue, enervate all our fortitude, and bring on a meanness and servility of spirit, so that we should easily become the dupes and abject slaves of despotism and tyranny. Indeed every sort of vice leads the way to both temporal and eternal slavery. But of all things ignorance opens the widest door to is; this paves the way to every vice, and disables a people from knowing the things of their temporal, as well as spiritual peace. How necessary therefore, to exert ourselves against all wickedness, and to promote all useful knowledge? But e're I am aware that I am carried too far here, and must return.

This question may require an answer.

What authority may be resisted?

I answer, unlawful authority, and all lawful officers acting unlawfully. There have been many officers, lawfully and well appointed, who have acted unlawfully in their office: and when this is the case, they should not be obeyed, but rather refitted in a due manner.

Officers are no better by nature than other men, and often have been worse by practice than those in a private sphere. I need not call in a Henry, a Stuart, a George, or a North to witness in the present case: we may find enough in this country since a Sir Edmund Andross, to prove the point. Such authority should be universally opposed with a manly firmness, and

an heroic virtue, until it be ended, and good and lawful authority established. But such wicked men are the first to plead *law* and *authority*, and to
cry out *rebellion* and *treason*, even when they are subverting the constitution, violating their solemn oaths, and depriving the people both of their
civil and religious rights. And if such men are not refitted we must obey man
rather than God. We must suffer all that is dear and valuable for soul and
body, for time and eternity, to be unjustly taken from us: We must give up to
lawless lust, ambition and tyranny; yea to despots and devils both. And can
we endure the thought? Let it rouse up every man, and excite a noble ardor
to blot the name of tyranny out of the land, and to keep up a steady firmness
and unshaken resolution to defend and support true liberty, and hand it
down to posterity as the best legacy we can bestow on them.

2. We infer the necessity of good rulers. *If the foundations be destroyed,
what can the righteous do?* A good constitution, good laws and good magistrates are very necessary to the well-being of a people. A state of anarchy is
ever a state of disorder and confusion. Injustice and every vice flourishes
with impunity, and no man's life or property is safe. How sad were the times
in Israel when they were without government? When the Levite's concubine
was forced 'till she was dead, we read, *In those days there was no king in
Israel; every man did that which was right in his own eyes* [Jud. 21:25].
There was no judge or supreme magistrate to put the laws in execution, and
the people were lawless. It is therefore evident that good rulers are necessary. Magistracy is an ordinance of God, and of great importance to the people.

Fourthly, is it as we have heard, that Jesus christ is the head and fountain of all authority? Hence we infer,

1. What a glorious and wonderful head of government we have. Jesus
Christ is the prince of the kings of the earth. When rulers have hearts after
his own heart; when they are sensible they derive their all from him; when
they heartily own him for their head and sovereign, pattern after him in
their lives, and copy his example in the execution of their offices, they are
blessings in their high stations, greatly useful to the State, and of vast importance to the people. But when they forget the Lord's anointed, Christ
their king, and let up themselves in his seat, and usurp his throne, they
become oppressors and lawless tyrants. O, but we, of all people in the world,
have cause to own and acknowledge the prince of peace to be our sovereign.

We have renounced the tyrant of Britain, and declaimed loudly against monarchical power; and have set up to be a free people. We own no other prince or sovereign but the prince of heaven, the great sovereign of the universe. To him we swear allegiance, and promise, through his abundant grace, to keep his laws.

The ten moral precepts are a brief summary of the whole law, the great law of nature. And the blessed Bible gives us a perfect comment upon it. Hence the scripture is too frequently called *The Law of the Lord.* Jesus Christ is the law-giver, and the commentator. And hence, as he is our maker, our king and our redeemer, we are bound to love, honor and obey him; to be subject to his law and government. We should receive his law as our rule and guide both in law-making and executing.

And truly we can be subject to none that is equal to him. O, his greatness! His transcendant excellence and glory! There is none like him for wisdom, for he is the wisdom of the father; and in him are hid all the treasures of wisdom and knowledge. He needs no counsel, for *counsel is his, and sound wisdom. His name is called wonderful, counselor.* There is none like him for power, for he is *the mighty God.* There is none like him for holiness, for he is *The holy one of Israel.* And concerning him the seraphims cry one to another, *holy, holy, holy is the Lord of hosts* [see Isa. 6:1–12 and compare it with John 12:39–41]. There is none like him for justice and righteousness, for *righteousness is the girdle of his loins.* There is none like him for goodness, for he is *the good shepherd.* There is none like him for truth, for he is the *verily, verily, the Amen, the faithful and true witnes.* There is none like him for mercy and kindness, for meekness and patience, for granting free access, for sympathy, for rewarding his faithful servants. There is none like him for riches and honors, for the multitude of subjects, and for largeness of territory and extensiveness of dominion. Surely there is no king like the king of America who lives and reigns forever and ever.

3. What a beautiful and lovely example have all rulers, even Jesus Christ the King of righteousness and peace! Jesus Christ is an example of impartial justice, and all his administrations are wise, good and gracious. He never took any bride, nor turned away the poor from his right. The rich and the poor are both alike to him. And they who upon any pretence whatever, neglect or refuse so noble a precedent, will find him a severe Judge at the last,

for to him all are accountable.

I now proceed to my second and last use.

II. A use of address to this venerable Audience upon this pleasing and joyful occasion.

Our eyes now see the foundation of a new republican state, laid on the noblest principles of true patriotism, religion and liberty, conspiring the temporal and eternal weal of present and future generation. And may heaven smile upon it appointing salvation for its walls and bulwarks!

In some respects we have suffered difficulties which no part of the United States of America have. We may therefore prize liberty the higher, and taste it the sweeter.

From the beginning of our settling in this late howling wilderness, we have groaned under British tyranny. How dark and gloomy that dismal day when their infant plantations fell under the jurisdiction of New York, whose officers being the tools of the crown, were no less arbitrary and cruel, in their unrighteous oppressions of our poor people, in the midst of all the natural and necessary hardships of a new settlement, than the savage tyrant of England their patron?

Our legal Charters have been demanded of us, whereby our lawful possessions have fallen into their unjust hands: and enormous sums demanded for their patents. Honest and virtuous people sued out of their proper inheritance; others driven to the last extremities by the force of the murderous arms. The most infamous men, who neither *feared God nor regarded man,* have been placed over us in the most important offices, from whom we could not expect mercy or justice.

As to religion, it seems to have been a thing least known or regarded in their courts and assemblies. And through the State the Lord's day has been, by a great part of rich and poor, a day of sports and recreations. No provision was made for the support of religion, but ministers have been left to all the hardships of a million among Savages, except the charities of a small number of more serious and good people whose lot fell among them. And truly such things must be very disagreeable to a virtuous people, brought up in the religious States of New-England, as the present inhabitants of this new State were. Such and much more, have been our troubles under the crown officers of that State. And the constitution and laws, since adopted by them, give the strongest evidence of the same arbitrary principles yet remaining. Blessed by God who has looked upon our affliction, and given us a happy deliverance from that iron yoke.

And when the enemy [General Bargoyne with about 10,000 British troops] came in like a flood upon us, the last summer and spread such scenes of horror and devastation, *the spirit of the Lord lifted up a standard against him:* so that after all his proud boasts and haughty insults, *he is fallen like Lucifer son of the morning.*

On this surprising and remarkable interposition of heaven, I would congratulate my country, the brave and worthy officers, and our valiant soldiers, who shewed a noble ardor and truly heroic spirit on the memorable sixteenth of August last, and thence afterward to the remarkable seventeenth of October, when British power and pride submitted to brave Americans. Then did the Lord *rise upon a cherub, and did fly; yea he did fly upon the wings of the wind* [Ps. 18:10]. Let us join the heavenly choir, *Alleluia, for the Lord God omnipotent reigneth* [Rev. 19:6]. But this was a salvation especially for this infant State, which we should record to the glory of our great deliverer.

And now, after laboring through inexpressible distress, divisions, and hardships, our joyful eyes see the foundation of a new State laid. O, may the superstructure be equal to it, and the blessing of the Lord rest upon it from generation to generation, that it may be a habitation of justice, a mountain of holiness, and a dwelling of peace and truth forever.

I would therefore in the name of our great King Jesus, humbly offer a word to our civil Fathers of this new State.

First to the Legislative Authority,

Truly worthy and most honored Gentlemen,

You have a most worthy and important part of the government assigned you, by the freemen of the State. Legislation requires great wisdom and skill. Laws should be framed and suitably adapted to the constitution, the necessities and conveniences of the people; very plain and explicit to prevent as much as possible, disputes, and that justice may be done in giving judgment.

And, Sirs, it is a new business you are called to work, which it is probable, you have been unused to, not have had but little opportunity to consider. With propriety therefore you may adopt the words of Solomon, and, in them, humbly address your great Lord, *I am but a little child, I know not how to go out, or come in—Give therefore thy servant an understanding heart* [1 Kings 3:7,9]. And we read, *The speech pleased the Lord.* Wisdom is necessary, and Christ our King says, *Counsel is mine and sound wisdom. In him are hid all the treasures of wisdom and knowledge;* you will, therefore, be entreated humbly and earnestly to apply yourselves to him for guidance in the paths of judgment; that, by his all-governing influence, he would furnish and assist you in the various branches of the very important business lying before you, and enable you to go through it, to the lasting good of the state, and your own honor and felicity.

And as Christ is your Lord and King, you will pay a due regard to his laws. You will be entreated to seek the true sense and spirit of them, heartily to believe and obey them, and to set them always before you as an excellent guide in the framing of every law for the State.

And how necessary it is, Sirs, that the best foundation be early laid for the suppression of every vice, and the encouragement of every virtue? And as ignorance is a great support of vice, and opens a wide door to temporal, ecclesiastical, and spiritual tyranny, you will wisely consider on the best means to promote the education of the rising generations in all useful knowledge. As also the encouragement and support of the ambassadors of Christ our King; that his religion and interest may be advanced to the present and future good of the people. Of what importance is this?

We heartily commend you, Sirs, to him that is able to keep you, and to guide you by his unerring counsel in the great work before you; so that it may hereafter be said of this State, in some good sense, as the inspired lawgiver of Israel, *What nation is there so great, that hath states and judgments so righteous as all their law?*

Secondly I would with all due deference address the Executive authority of the State.

Worthy and honored gentlemen,

You are God's ministers. Dread title! The sword you wear is the sword of the Lord; the sword of justice to keep the peace to the State, and of each part within your province. The eyes of all, within the State, look up to you for justice. And may the supreme Executive power, and all our judges and justices of the peace keep in view the infinitely great and supreme Judge *by whom all the judges of the earth do rule,* and ever shake their hands from holding bribes.

Permit me, Sirs, to say we expect, and, what is inconceivably greater, Christ our sovereign expects that each of you be terror to evil doers, and a praise to them that do well.

We trust the honorable Legislature will furnish you with good and wholesome laws, without which we cannot expect you can do much. And may we hope, Gentlemen, that the general complaint of which has been long in England, and in all parts of this country, more or less, may never be heard among us, *The want of justice.*

No man can number all the good and wholesome laws that have been made in England and the country against all sorts of vice, and that justice might be done for the public, and between man and man; and yet how has vice appeared with its brazen face, in open effrontery of all law and justice? And what multitudes have suffered for want of a speedy execution of justice? And the public has suffered through a careless negligence, bribes, vicious rulers, or the artifices of bribed and perjured attorneys.

May heaven prevent such abuses among us! And may you, Gentlemen, and your successors, nobly exert yourselves to do justice and judgment. How worthy the practical observation of all rulers is the charge of good Jehoshaphat? *And he said to the judges, Take heed what you do, for ye judge not for men, but for the Lord who is with you in the judgment. Wherefore now, let the fear of the Lord be upon you: take heed and do it, for there is no iniquity with the Lord our God, nor respect of persons, nor taking of gifts.—Thus shall ye do in the fear of the Lord faithfully, and with a perfect heart* [2 Chron. 19:6–10]. We wish you much wisdom and fortitude, and heartily pray you may go on and prosper in the impartial administration of justice and judgment, and that you may *have boldness in the day of Christ.*

Thirdly, I would, in the next place, address the freemen of the State.

Gentlemen, you are as free citizens, and the whole power of the State falls yearly into your hands. Remember the solemn oath you have taken in the great name of the ever living God, and be not swayed by interest, party or prejudice, in giving your suffrages.

If you have a proper sense of the great importance and worth of your priviloges, you will look for men of God, *men of truth, able men, such as fear God and hate covetousness,* and give your votes for such from time to time.

A good constitution all Liberty worth the name, and every thing dear and sacred may soon be subverted by wicked designing men, who are ever gaping for places of preferment and profit.

It is a great deal you put into the hands of your representatives. And men of no virtue, no principle or conscience cannot be trusted, but with the greatest peril.

And be entreated, Sirs, to seek the peace and prosperity of your towns, and of the whole State: and labor to promote and encourage every virtue among yourselves, and the suppression of every vice. And, of what importance is it to yourselves and prosperity, that your houses be nurseries of piety and devotion? As also, that you spare not to educate your children in useful learning and the principles of our holy religion? Like faithful Abraham, *command your children and your households after you to keep the way of the Lord, to do justice and judgment* [Gen. 18:19].

And how necessary is it, dear Sirs, that you settle able and faithful ministers of Christ in your several towns; that you and your children may enjoy a preached gospel, and all its ordinances and institutions according to the mind of Christ. And remember for your encouragement that *Blessed are the people that know the joyful sound* [Ps. 115:15–17].

Once more, and above all, I beseech you to bow to our glorious sovereign prince. And may Christ our King reign in your hearts, in his sweet and benign influence! May he be crowned King upon the throne of your souls, and sway his sweet and peaceful scepter there forever! Happy it would be to see his kingdom of grace flourishing in this State; and many flocking round his standard. Christ reigns in providence, and in grace: and he is almighty, he is lovely in both. How glorious is that kingdom which consists in righteousness, peace and joy in the Holy Ghost? How transcendently amiable and lovely the King of glory, by whom kings reign, having all power in heaven and in earth! *Thy kingdom come.*

Fourthly, I would offer a word to my Reverend brethren in the ministry. [The Address to the Ministers, omitted in Delivery, by reason, that none of the ministers of the State were present, takes its place in the Publication.]

Reverend and dear Sirs,

It is a peculiarly sweet consideration to us that our divine Lord and Master has *all power in heaven and in earth,* and for this very purpose *that he should give eternal life to as many as the Father has given him* [John 17:2]. This is the great end of his providential government. And as he is able so he will most certainly accomplish it. He will govern all things, all nations and all occurrences in providence of every name and nature, so as to conduce to the bringing home his people in a thorough conversion, and their final and complete glorification.

We have but little encouragement from visibility to present. All things outward look dark. It is a dark day on account of the unnatural war: a darker on account of the great wickedness of the country. Alas! The drunkenness, profanity, uncleanness and Sabbath breaking through the land. O, what a lamentable decay of vital piety, family religion and government! How seldom do we find any inquiring the way to Zion! The spirit of conviction and conversion seems apparently to have left the country and almost universally. The wise virgins are slumbering and sleeping with the foolish. Such an impenetrable hardness of hearts prevails, that no judgments of heaven seem to make any impression on the wicked, but every day they grow more obdurate and insensible. The most awakening, melting and alarming discourses from the sacred desk are rather derided than regarded. Surely, these things are heavy on the hearts of Christ's ministers. But although Satan rages, *the Lord reigns.*

And now my brethren how are we? What sense have we of these things? Have we let down our watch with others? Can we content ourselves without the spirit and energy of religion in our own souls, and to see it prevailing among the people? O, why are we not up in good earnest? Why are we not importunate in our prayers? Pungent and pressing in our applications? Unwearied in our labors night and day? Surely there is enough in Christ, enough in his sweet promises to encourage and strengthen our faith, *Lo, I am with you always, even to the end of the world. I will not leave you comfortless. I will come unto you, I will pour water upon him that is thirsty, and floods upon the dry ground: I will pour my spirit upon thy seed, and my blessing upon thine offspring.* We may therefore look for great things from our Lord. And in due time we shall reap if we faint not.

One more thing I would observe, *The laborers are few,* very few in this infant State, and at present but little prospect of many additions. Let us pray the Lord of the harvest to send forth laborers into his harvest. And while there is such a paucity of ministers in the State, are we not called in providence, to double our labors among the people scattered in the wilderness as sheep without a shepherd?

It is indeed sadly true that many appear to have but little regard to the ministry, having gross errors and corrupt opinions, contrary to the doctrine which is according to godliness. Yet, in dependence upon our great Lord and Master, we may be instrumental of winning some to Christ, and of preventing many more from following their pernicious ways.

We cannot prevent diversity of opinions, or the grossest errors, neither can the State. Our part is faithfully to deliver all the counsel of God in public and in private, and to commit all to our sovereign Lord, in a quiet resignation to his will. He governs all things civil and religious.

We cannot reasonably desire but that every one enjoy the free liberty of his conscience. It is nevertheless evident that many abuse it. Yea they abuse both their civil and religious liberty yet we should rejoice that there is such a precious privilege granted us. And after using our best endeavors, they must be left to their own master, to whom they stand or fall. God is the Judge.

It is a very plain case that many people in the present day, have very absurd notions of Liberty, as if it consisted in a right for every one to beleive, do or act as he pleases in all things civil and religious. This is a *Libertine* principle. No man has any right, before God, to believe or practice contrary to scripture. And Liberty consists in a freedom to do that which is right. The great law of nature, the moral law, is the rule of right action. This is the rule of moral and civil liberty. Man's fall has taken away his freedom of right action; for *whosoever committeth sin is the servant of sin.* In the kingdom of providence Christ gives a civil freedom: in the kingdom of grace he gives a spiritual freedom. The Gospel is *the perfect Law of Liberty;* and this lays the foundation for a perfect moral freedom. It is the spiritual freedom we are especially concerned to seek among the people. And for this we should labor with the greatest painfulness.

How sorrowful, that a free people, in a civil sense should be the servants and slaves of sin and Satan? O that he who was anointed to proclaim liberty to the captives, are the opening of the prison to them that are bound would speedily accomplish this happy deliverance, and most glorious freedom! Let us pray for the peace of Jerusalem. And may the blessing of many that are ready to perish come upon us.

AMEN.